Commentary On The Revelation Of Jesus Christ

Handley H. Edlin

ACKNOWLEDGEMENTS AND THANKS TO:

- The Rolling Fork Christian Church Adult Bible School Class, for asking me to teach the book of Revelation, and the elders, for allowing me to teach it (9/97 – 3/98).

- Roy Donahue, for taping each session and making sure the tape recorder was working properly each Sunday.

- Sheila Lyvers, for buying and delivering the tapes.

- My daughter, Dana Edlin, for typing twenty-nine lessons from the tapes.

- My wife, Jane, for editing the lessons.

- My daughter, Anita Cooper, for retyping and proof-reading the manuscript.

I hope this work will benefit everyone who is studying the Word of God and I hope it can help the end-time Christians who will be searching for anything that will give hope and encouragement.

The Revelation of Jesus Christ

- The English word, Revelation, is a translation of the Greek word, Apocalypse.
- The meaning of the word: to show or expose to view.
- The scribe of Revelation was the apostle John.
- The true Author of the Book is God.
- The subject: to expose to view the nature of Jesus Christ – past, present, and future.
- The Book of Revelation covers the entire Church Age.

CHAPTER 1

1. *The Revelation of Jesus Christ, which God gave unto him, to shew unto his servants things which must shortly come to pass; and he sent and signified it by his angel unto his servant John:*
2. *Who bare record of the word of God, and of the testimony of Jesus Christ, and of all things that he saw.*
3. *Blessed is he that readeth, and they that hear the words of this prophecy, and keep those things which are written therein: for the time is at hand.*
4. *John to the seven churches which are in Asia: Grace be unto you, and peace, from him which is, and which was, and which is to come; and from the seven Spirits which are before his throne;*

This prophecy of Jesus Christ was given to the apostle John as authorized by the Godhead…the Father, Son, and Holy Spirit. John was to record these prophecies for the present and future generations…things that would soon begin to happen. The apostle John was referred to as a servant of Jesus Christ. He gave first hand testimony of all things the Holy Spirit revealed to him.

It is good to know all we can about things that will affect us. If we plan to visit a country that we know nothing about and someone is nice enough to tell us about this place, about the blessings there for every child of God, it would certainly make us happy. Happiness is also for those who hear the Words of this prophecy, which means pay attention and understand that all these happenings will be brought forth at the time appointed by the Lord God.

Jesus' death, burial, and resurrection was the beginning of a new relationship brought about according to the promises of God. This fulfilled His plan of redemption.

We learn from the Bible that mercy and forgiveness, in the name of Jesus Christ, was extended first to the Jews, who were present at Jerusalem, when Peter preached the first sermon. We learn that the same Jesus, whom they had crucified (Acts 2:35-40), was Lord and Savior, Son of God, just like He said He was. We learn from studying the Bible that the only way back into the family of God is through Him:

- First, by believing His Word (Acts 8:37).
- By faith, doing what it says (Romans 10:17).
- Repenting of our sins (Acts 17:30). We are children of Adam. Adam sinned. We were in him when he sinned and we have inherited his likeness.
- Confessing Jesus as the Divine Son of God (Acts 8:37). He then confesses us before the Father in Heaven.
- Being baptized by immersion in water as He commanded and for what He promised (Acts 2:38, 42). That is, forgiveness of sins and the gift of the Holy Spirit. Then, being a child of God, remaining faithful to the apostles' doctrine.

If you do not know Jesus as your Lord and Savior, find a believer as soon as possible and tell him you want to obey the plan of salvation. Do not delay. The time is at hand.

5. And from Jesus Christ, who is the faithful witness, and the first begotten of the dead, and the prince of

the kings of the earth. Unto Him that loved us, and washed us from our sins in his own blood.
6. *And hath made us kings and priests unto God and His Father; to Him be glory and dominion forever and ever. Amen.*

John is addressing seven churches in Asia. He later names the seven churches in chapters two and three. We do know there were these seven cities and that there was a church located within the boundary of each city.

The number seven represents one hundred percent. I believe the Holy Spirit wants us to understand that this prophecy is for the church universally; since we know that at the time these seven existed there were many more churches.

The words of warning that He gives to correct the problems are on going and have proven to be continually needed for correction.

He who was, who is and has promised to return, is Jesus Christ. He is a faithful witness. He is the first to be raised from the dead. Jesus is the best King that has ever been known by people on the earth. He loved us before we loved Him. He forgives us of our sins...all that are obedient to Him. He has allowed us to be adopted children of God through contacting His blood. Life is in the blood (Leviticus 17:11). Through Adam we lost blood that had life. By faith, we contact the blood of Christ (Romans 6:3, 4), which has life, and we then are of the bloodline of our Father, God. We are restored again to the family of God. This way God protects His justice system. Jesus made it possible for us to be royal priests of God, His Father. As royal priests we can pray and be heard by our Father in heaven. We can give ourselves as a sacrifice and of our substance that represents a part of us.

7. *Behold, he cometh with clouds; and every eye shall see him, and they also which pierced him: and all*

*kindreds of the earth shall wail because of him. Even
so, Amen.*

8. *I am Alpha and Omega, the beginning and the ending,
saith the Lord, which is, and which was, and which is
to come, the Almighty.*

9. *I John, who also am your brother, and companion in
tribulation, and in the kingdom and patience of Jesus
Christ, was in the isle that is called Patmos, for the
word of God, and for the testimony of Jesus Christ.*

When Jesus comes at the final judgment all people that
have not known Him as Lord and Savior will be resurrected from their graves and will know Him and witness
His appearing. They will wail when they hear their eternal
condemnation being announced by Him as He says, *depart
from me. I never knew you.*

Jesus (the Word) was there in the beginning and took part
in creating all things. He has been involved with the devel-
opment of everything that is good. He will also be present
when the end of all things comes.

The apostle John overcame many tribulations. He knew
what it was to be persecuted for faith in Jesus. He suffered
many things because of his dedication to the kingdom of
God. The world hated what he stood for. That is why he was
a prisoner on the lonely island called Patmos. The enemy of
Christ knew John would tell others about Him if he were free
to do so. The apostle John was given a measure of the Holy
Spirit that enabled him to receive instructions from heaven
and record them for future generations.

These special messengers (the apostles) were never to be
succeeded. In other words, there would never be any other
men thus equipped, nor would there need to be, since they
received the final, complete message from God. This way it
is the same instruction for every generation that has lived or
will live on God's earth.

*10. I was in the Spirit on the Lord's day, and heard behind
me a great voice, as of a trumpet,*

John identifies the day that this Revelation came to him…
the Lord's Day. The method used, to reveal these things to
John, was unmistakably clear…the voice of God.

I want to make some comments about the last half of the
fourth verse.

And from the seven Spirits which are before His throne;

Let's look at Isaiah, chapter 11:1, 2:

*And there shall come forth a rod out of the stem of Jesse,
and a branch shall grow out of his roots: And the spirit of
the Lord shall rest upon him, the spirit of wisdom and understanding, the spirit of counsel and might, the spirit of knowledge and of the fear of the Lord;*

We have here multiple titles. It is a fair assumption,
concerning the Holy Spirit of God, that this is a reference to
the seven-fold work of the Holy Spirit. In the book of Isaiah
we find light being shed on this passage of scripture.

God has given us the ability to think. He has given us
things to consider. He does not chew, swallow, and digest it
for us. When we go to the table for food, we help ourselves,
take the food, and ingest it into our body. God wants us to
ingest His Word into our mind. It gives us a challenge to do
this. It makes us feel proud to be able to take things God has
given us and sort them out.

I will be using the King James translation of the Bible
throughout because people are familiar with it. Not because
I think it is more perfect than any other, but I believe something familiar, when dealing with a subject such as this, is
what I should stay with.

11. Saying, I am Alpha and Omega, the first and the last: and, What thou seest, write in a book, and send it unto the seven churches which are in Asia; unto Ephesus, and unto Smyrna, and unto Pergamos, and unto Thyatira, and unto Sardis, and unto Philadelphia, and unto Laodicea.

The gospel had been preached, during the apostle's era of time, to the entire known world. It might be interesting to note that it has not been done since. We pray that once again it can be extended to the entire world.

As we look at the Alpha and Omega, First and Last, this tells us of the eternality of Jesus Christ...not only Jesus Christ, but also the Godhead – Father, Son, and Holy Spirit. They always are, and always will be. This denotes strength, because the first and last is always the most powerful. Jesus says, *I am Alpha and Omega – the First and Last.* Jesus tells John to write this Revelation in a book.

In the computer age of today we have such high tech ways of corresponding that many my age cannot imagine. We can send mail and messages around the world almost instantaneously. But in John's day they only had a form of writing – something that was legible. This is what God wanted John to do, make something legible and permanent that could be sent out to the churches.

When we look at the churches are we going to assume that God is only interested in seven churches? No, we cannot think like that. This would not be wise for us to think that God is only interested in seven churches in seven cities. Our mind must think and rethink this subject. He said write it to the seven churches and He named the churches that we do know existed. We know there were many more in addition to the seven. As we see only seven names given, how can we say that God shows no favoritism? We know that God does not show favoritism; therefore, He is not interested in only the seven churches named here. He is interested in all the churches. The number seven is a complete number with God. Seven names, seven churches, is to be understood that God is directing this message to all churches that were in existence at that time. As we look further we will also find that he wanted it to go to every church of every age.

> *12. And I turned to see the voice that spake with me. And being turned, I saw seven golden candlesticks;*
> *13. And in the midst of the seven candlesticks one like unto the Son of man, clothed with a garment down to the foot, and girt about the paps with a golden girdle.*
> *14. His head and his hairs were white like wool, as white as snow; and his eyes were as a flame of fire;*
> *15. And his feet like unto fine brass, as if they burned in a furnace; and his voice as the sound of many waters.*

We read in verse 13...*in the midst of the seven candlesticks one like the Son of Man clothed...* The candlesticks represent the gospel. The only light for this world is the Light that comes through Jesus Christ. The churches are the bearers of the Light, but the source is from God. The Light must come from the Word of God. It doesn't matter how high we are on the pyramid of authority we cannot be the source.

A good description of that is...we pour oil into a bowl, put a wick down into the oil, we then light the wick, and it burns. If we examine the light closely we see that the source of the light is from the oil that is in the bowl.

God is the oil that gives the Light. We are the ones that shed the Light. We show forth the Light into the world, as Christians. We must never forget this. We live on this earth to spread the Light of the gospel. God says that every church, every Christian, has the Light and He wants that Light to shine to the lost world. The church is made up of Christian people and the people are the church. We must not forget that wherever we go, whatever we do, we are torchbearers for the Lord Jesus Christ.

And I turned to see the voice that spoke with me. And being turned, I saw seven golden candlesticks; and in the midst of the seven candlesticks one like unto the Son of man, clothed with a garment down to the foot, and girt about the paps with a golden girdle.

We know that John was very familiar with Jesus Christ. The description John gives is the identification of Jesus.

As we said in the beginning, this is a Revelation of Jesus Christ. We know that many attributes of Jesus have already been revealed. When we finish this study of the book of Revelation we are going to know who He is. We know Him as Savior, we know He is kind and merciful, but He is also powerful and that is what the study of Revelation will reveal. He is a powerful individual and too awesome for our mind to even comprehend.

*...clothed with a garment down to the foot...*What does this remind us of as we think of the Mosaical dispensation and the Levitical priesthood? The dress of the high priest was different from the rest of the people. Jesus Christ is our high priest, so we are all priests, in a sense, under Him. This tells us what John saw and that he is describing Jesus as the High Priest because of His dress. When we study the Old Testament we see that as the high priests ministered in the temple they wore a long skirt down to the feet.

*...a golden girdle...*This is a symbol of power.

The *white hair*, in verse 14, reminds us of His eternality. It tells us that Jesus is eternal, like no other that has lived in human form. Jesus lived before He took on human form. He limited Himself to human frailties. Not because He had to, but because He came to be our Savior. His white hair reminds us of the eternal God, of His righteousness...complete righteousness. As Christians, we put on the righteousness of Jesus Christ. The Bible refers to this as dressed in white.

...eyes were as a flame of fire;... This reminds us that there is no hiding from Jesus...that His eyes can see through any form. As Jesus can see the whole Church Age, we find here His indignation. What is He angry about? You mean Jesus gets angry? Yes, He does. This is another Revelation of Jesus Christ. He is angry because He can see that the church, throughout the Church Ages, is not following the pattern He has given. This causes Him to have indignation. The eyes of indignation are because of the apostate church and the apostate Church Ages that we know have existed on this earth and continue to exist today. When the teaching is not according to the Word of God, He is angry.

We cannot understand the book of Revelation without knowing the rest of the Bible, especially the Old Testament. I will make some references as we go along, but you will need to study to find things in the Bible that will help you to understand what these words are as Jesus is being described.

And his feet like unto fine brass... This reminds us of the brazen altar in the temple where sin was judged. John is giving a description of Jesus as being a judge.

Revelation is written in a wonderful way. You may say, "I wonder about that." Once you have studied it long enough you will not forget it. Something we are told, just "off the cuff," without putting some time to it can be easily forgotten. I cannot remember things without giving them a lot of time, thought, and study.

...his voice as the sound of many waters. What could John be referring to here? He could not use a jet airplane as an example because it had not been invented. There is one thing we can all understand and that is the sound of many waters. As I stood by Niagara Falls once, I found it impos-

sible to talk to anyone. You cannot hear another thing. ... *his voice as the sound of many waters...* He wants all other voices, when it comes to the spiritual realm of our life, to be blotted out. We must know when the teaching is not coming from the Word of God. We must hear Him and Him only.

16. And he had in his right hand seven stars:

The seven stars, according to Revelation 1:20, are the angels. This word from the oldest Greek manuscripts should have been translated "messenger" in the English word. There is only one true and trustworthy messenger and that is the Holy Spirit.

But the Comforter, which is the Holy Spirit, whom the Father will send in my name, he shall teach you all things, and bring all things to your remembrance, whatsoever I have said unto you (John 14:26).

According to Isaiah 11:21, we have multiple descriptions of His power and His titles.

...and out of his mouth went a sharp two-edged sword: and his countenance was as the sun shineth in his strength.

In Ephesians 6:17, the Word of God is pointed out as being the Sword of the Spirit. In Hebrews 4:12, the Holy Spirit tells us that the Word of God is *sharper than any two-edged sword.*

17. And when I saw him, I fell at his feet as dead. And he laid his right hand upon me, saying unto me, Fear not; I am the first and the last:

We know that the one with the great power prevails.

18. I am he that liveth, and was dead; and behold, I am alive for evermore, Amen; and have the keys of hell and of death.

The *keys of hell*, means He has power to judge and condemn. The *keys of death*, means He has power to save and to deliver from the sentence of death. All human beings are under the sentence that was pronounced on Adam and his descendants when he disobeyed God.

19. Write the things which thou hast seen, and the things which are, and the things which shall be hereafter;

Jesus is telling John to write the Revelation and make a permanent record of it. He means that He will not reveal this to any other man, that John's record will be important for succeeding generations.

John is also told what the future holds for the people, the events that will come to pass here on the earth, concluding with the judgment of the wicked and the establishment of the eternal order for the saved.

20. The mystery of the seven stars which thou sawest in my right hand, and the seven golden candlesticks. The seven stars are the angels of the seven churches: and the seven candlesticks which thou sawest are the seven churches.

The candlesticks being the Light for the world, the church has the only true Light.

We must be able to see farther than just a few years here on earth. Many people are putting all of their life into developing themselves for less than eighty years – then the end. Unless we have more light than that, we will not have much to look forward to.

The church shows forth the Light that shines into eternity. The church has the only Light that shines into eternity.

God gives us Light to see, as far as we need to, while we are on this earth.

I heard an example one time that I have not forgotten. Sometimes you hear illustrations and they really do ring a bell with you. This one did for me. The fellow giving the example said, "You start out with your car, turn your lights on, and you see down the road so many yards. As you begin to drive, the light just keeps on extending." That is the way our faith in God is. Our faith just keeps on extending for us. It gives us the Light we need as we go through this life and then we will be able to see eternity.

I have put a lot of time on this one verse. At least twenty percent of my time, in studying the book of Revelation, was on this one verse of scripture because it is not easy to understand. I will do the best I can. I do not want to do disservice to the Word of God or lead God's people astray in any way whatsoever.

*...the angels of the seven churches...*The Greek word angelos (meaning messenger) is translated angels in our English Bibles. Vine's dictionary, on the meaning of the Greek word says, "Angels are spirits, they have not material bodies as men have – they can assume the human form when necessary." We can eliminate the thought that this scripture may be referring to man because man is fallible. Our conclusion must be that the "angels of the seven churches" is the Holy Spirit of God. The Holy Spirit that Christ sent to be with us does more than guide us through the Word of God. I have heard some people refer to the Holy Spirit as being the Word. The Word is the message of the Holy Spirit, but we must not confine the Holy Spirit to the Word. He comes to live in our lives by the promise of God. I believe that the Holy Spirit is in my life and I believe that He is in your life as you are obeying God. He has to be more than a word. He

is the Word, but He is more than the Word and He is more than the personification of good. We may see someone and say they are good and they do good things, but the Holy Spirit is more than that. He works in a way that we know He is aiding and assisting us as we live and are willing to obey Him. We can grieve Him. He will depart from us if we grieve Him long enough. He lives in each Christian, as he or she is obedient to God's Word. In John 16:7-13, Jesus said, *He will guide you in all truth.*

In Romans 8:16, we find the apostle Paul saying that the Holy Spirit bears witness with our spirit. If the wording said to our spirit then someone could say He bore witness to me of such and such, but that is not the wording. The wording is "with." The word with means that He bears witness with everyone with the same message. He does not deviate. He does not discriminate. He bears witness with our spirit.

With all the things I find in the Bible of the messenger from heaven I must conclude that He is the Holy Spirit of God. He has been active in the world since the establishment of the church. We cannot be developed any other way except through His message. The Bible says that we are to be drawn to God through His Word, through His message. We might say to ourselves, as we look at the seven churches, how can that be? How can it be that the Holy Spirit is the "angels" since the angels did not keep their churches pure? As we study the churches we find they have not been kept pure. How can that be the Holy Spirit? The Holy Spirit would have a pure message from God. Bear in mind that God did not give Him power to supersede the will of man. God does not use His power to supersede our will. The Bible says that He loves us. John 3:16 says...*so much that He sent His only begotten Son that whosoever believes in Him should not perish but have everlasting life.* We find that the Bible says the majority of people will be lost. It says *wide is the gate, and broad is the way, that leads to destruction, and many there be which go in thereat: ...strait is the gate, and narrow is the way, which leadeth unto life, and few there be that find it* (Matthew 7:13,14). God has not superseded the will of man nor will He do that. He has chosen a way to convert us by appealing to us through our will and our freedom of choice. Christ has subjected himself to being outside our hearts because He said, *Behold I stand at your hearts door and knock* – I just knock. God, Jesus Christ, or the Holy Spirit does not supersede the will of man. They simply appeal through the written, Holy Spirit inspired, Word of God.

We will go through the seven churches again. We know there were more than the seven churches and seven cities mentioned. There was not just a´ problem in the seven churches named. There was a problem that every one of the churches in existence needed to look at.

The gospel had been preached throughout the known world at that time. Everyone was not converted to Jesus Christ, but many people did accept Him as Lord and Savior.

We have seven churches mentioned that were in John's day and we have seven divisions of church history. Notice the chart at the end of this chapter – all seven are listed there. Note the insignia over each one.

Ephesus: The cloven tongues of fire identify the Apostolic Church Age. It lasted from A.D. 33 to A.D. 100 – this may not be exactly to the day.

Smyrna: The Persecuted Church Age was next.

Fox's Book of Martyrs is a recommended book in Christendom today – it is accurate. It tells us that the mass killings of Christians was prior to A.D. 313 and gives an estimate of millions of Christians being killed during the period of A.D. 100 through A.D. 312.

22

The church did better, flourished more, had more converts, and more people were dedicated to God during the Persecuted Church Age than ever before – it grew faster.

Pergamum: The Indulged Church Age.

Do you know what Satan did during this period of time? He reversed his tactics. He must have said, "This is not working – I'm going to stop my attack on the church. I'm going to make sure the church people are blessed; that they have freedom in everything."

Bear in mind that during this period of time there were no divisions in the church like we know today. All during this period and until the Protestant Reformation there was never anything like denominational divisions. It all operated as the church.

The Pergamum Church Age, A.D. 312 to A.D. 606, was a long period of time – close to three hundred years. Notice the flag – it was a State religion. People came to America because they wanted freedom – freedom of worship. They did not feel that the State church was providing any such freedom.

Thyatira: The Pagan Church Age.

Whenever you have something like forced religion and a State religion, it is open for corruption. Everyone has to be a member of it and when you get unconverted people in as members it is open for paganism. So paganism was reintroduced into the church. Teachings brought into the church by pagans were not even close to what the apostles taught or what was recorded in the Bible. The pagans began to attack the Holy Spirit inspired message.

Beginning with the State run church, we have the teachers of Baal and Nicolaitan's. I'll do a little explaining on this later.

When we go to the Old Testament we find a person named Jezebel. She more or less wanted to run everything when she married the king. When the king wanted something, if he didn't have enough courage to get it, she did. She would kill or do whatever necessary. She introduced paganism into the temple worship.

The Pagan Thyatira Church Age imitated Jezebel in teaching idolatry. They sacrificed unto the pagan gods as well as to the One True God of Israel. God did not like that. He did not want them to worship pagan gods and then say, "Now we don't want to forget the God of Israel." They probably did not call Him the One True God because they believed the pagan gods were just as good.

Do you remember, from studying the Old Testament, how Elijah and Jezebel had a contest (I Kings 18)? Elijah rebelled against pagan worship being done beside the worship of the One True God. Elijah said to the prophets of Baal, "Prepare your sacrifice first and call on the name of your gods." The pagan prophets prepared their sacrifice and called out to their gods, but could not get a response because there were no gods. Elijah built an altar in the name of the Lord and the people did all that he told them to do. God then, before them all, proved that He was the One True God.

Paganism was reintroduced during this Pagan Thyatira Church Age. The insignia is the cathedral. From that day to this there has not been an end to the pagan mixture in the religious world.

Sardis: The Dead Church Age.

On the chart the insignia is death. This was around A.D. 1520 and was called the dark ages. Do you know why it was called the dark ages? Because Satan decided the Bible should not be open to the layman. He separated the clergy and layman and said the clergy are the only ones who can understand the Bible. Let them interpret it to the layman. This of course became the Dead Church Age. I do not believe there has ever been a time on this earth when there have not been some faithful believers. But I think they were few during this Church Age.

Philadelphia: The Back to the Bible Church Age.

The 1700's are not so far away that you and I cannot have some pretty good history of this. If you study books in regard to the Restoration Movement and those associated with the Movement you will find that it was in the late 1700's when it had its beginning. They were searching for the Truth – nothing but the Truth. This became the church that Jesus commended. He had nothing against it, but He said it was weak. What does He mean by being weak? It could not have been weak in Spirit because He commended it too highly. You have to eliminate the thought that it was weak in that way. It was strong in that way, but small in number.

Laodicea: The Lukewarm Church Age.

The Philadelphia Church Age goes into the Laodicea Church Age. Each church age has to blend into the other.

As society changes, as our public school system changes, as our government changes, so does the church. I have heard several preachers say the structure of the church and the government of the church is a lot like the government of the countries. Why? Because we become familiar with the structure of our government and when we go into the church it is, more or less, set up by the same principle. We may not intend for it to be that way, but it becomes that way.

The Laodicean Church has less commendation than all the other churches.

The Jewish element of the church preached the gospel to the known world in less than fifty years. That is quite an achievement. They did not have radio, television, or printed page.

Seven being the whole, then the command was to go to all churches of that day with the gospel message that had been revealed to the apostles by the Holy Spirit.

I believe it was at, or immediately after, the death of the last apostle that the devil probably said, "I'm going to have a hay-day." Because those inspired witnesses that had a measure of the Holy Spirit to speak Truth were gone. Bear in mind there were people they had chosen to lay their hands on, to convey gifts upon. Not all the gifts they possessed, but gifts of tongues, interpretation, prophecy...those people still existed. They were still living. They were an easier mark for Satan to attack. He could attack the validity of what they said much easier than he could the apostles.

Paul went back to Jerusalem, as you will find recorded in chapter fifteen of the Book of Acts, and He met with the elders of the church including Peter and the others. They reviewed everything Paul was doing and acknowledged his Divine leading. That was the first attack by Satan on the church. But do you think he stopped because the first one didn't work? He came back and attacked the church again and again. He has caused seven major divisions in Christendom. These are not petty things, but they are the major elements causing division in the Christian world. I hate for Christendom to be divided. I am not talking about the Restoration Movement; I am talking about Christendom. We need to remove the cause.

I love people that may not see things exactly like I do. You might say, "He doesn't love them – he acts like he hates them." No, I do not hate them. I would spend any amount of time to go and talk with them, but not to force my opinion on them. My opinion is no more important than someone

26

else's...but God's Word is. We have to put our personal belief aside and go with the Word in order to remove division from Christendom. That is all I think anyone should do. If our belief doesn't measure up with the Word we have to let it go without reservation.

Here are some things that divide Christians today:

- Apostolic authority
- Apostolic succession
- Works
- Grace
- Miracles
- Tradition
- Failing to rightly divide the Word of Truth

This is not Bible, but my opinion. This is what I see as I have talked and debated various ministers of different denominations. I never debated a minister of a different faith without first praying to God that I would try my best to love his soul and that I would be bold enough to stand up for the Truth. We are not past the time of debate. We must defend the gospel! Since when are we supposed to say that it is time to stop defending the gospel? We are not to get in "lock-step" with people who say we are out of the era of debate. Discussing our belief of the Word of God is good. It can be very enlightening for anyone, but we must do it in love.

As we think of the seven churches we need to see their problems and say to ourselves, "Do I have the problem?" I pray to God that if I do have the problem I will see it and try to remove it.

THE SEVEN CHURCH AGES OF REVELATION BEGINNING WITH PENTECOST

EPHESUS	SMYRNA	PERGAMUM	THYATIRA	SARDIS	PHILADELPHIA	LAODICEA
The Apostolic Church	*The Persecuted Church*	*The Indulged Church*	*The Pagan Church*	*The Dead Church*	*Back To The Bible*	*The Lukewarm Church*
A.D. 33 - 100	A.D. 100 - 312	A.D. 312 - 606	A.D. 606 - 1520	A.D. 1520 - 1776	A.D. 1776-1974	A.D. 1974 -
Apostolic Age - Word of God revealed to the apostles. Church created.	Mass killings of Christians because of their faith. According to Fox's Book of Martyrs, 7 million were killed.	Priest required money donated to the church for right to sin. Some sins greater than others - more money.	State or Government controlled church. Dark Age - very few true Christians.	Thou art dead - works not complete. Protestant Reformation, toward end of church age.	Restoration Movement - return to primitive church. Apostles doctrine - nothing added, nothing taken away. Small in number.	Luke warm - everyone choosing their own belief. Apostles doctrine not important. Nicolaitanism accepted.

CHAPTER 2

1. *Unto the angel of the church of Ephesus write; These things saith he that holdeth the seven stars in his right hand, who walketh in the midst of the seven golden candlesticks;*
2. *I know thy works, and thy labour, and thy patience, and how thou canst not bear them which are evil; and thou hast tried them which say they are apostles, and are not, and has found them liars:*
3. *And hast borne, and hast patience, and for my name's sake hast laboured, and hast not fainted.*
4. *Nevertheless I have somewhat against thee, because thou hast left thy first love.*
5. *Remember therefore from whence thou art fallen, and repent and do the first works; or else I will come unto thee quickly, and will remove thy candlestick out of his place, except thou repent.*
6. *But this thou hast, that thou hatest the deeds of the Nicolaitans, which I also hate.*
7. *He that hath an ear, let him hear what the Spirit saith unto the churches; To him that overcometh will I give to eat of the tree of life, which is in the midst of the paradise of God.*

We find something here that Jesus commended them for. He said, "You have put Nicolaitanism down and defeated it.

You hate it, I hate it." We are pleasing Jesus Christ if we hate Nicolaitanism and we will talk about what that is.

Many people have gone down the aisle weeping because of the spiritual condition they were in. They are so happy to be a Christian that the very next Sunday they are back on the front seat ready to hear God's Word and worship Him.

We go to church to worship God...not the preacher or the teacher. We do not have hierarchy in the church. We do not have anyone that we must bow down before. There is no such thing in the church of the Lord Jesus Christ. We are on a level playing field. We are here to worship God and there should never be anything in the church to keep us from doing that.

The Apostolic Church left their first love. They had become so comfortable with Christianity in the world. They did not keep the Spirit renewed within them like we must do as we worship and pray to God.

Pray without ceasing! Someone said, "You cannot pray constantly." We can have Jesus on our mind as we go about our daily activities. I think that is what He meant. We will not depart from our first love if we do that. The best way to depart from our first commitment to the Lord Jesus Christ is to become distracted by things in the world.

The devil says, "Look at them! They're doing this in church and that in church – you might as well not go." The devil has people posted all over. He has husbands telling wives, "Don't go to church." He has wives telling husbands, "Don't go to church, they're doing this and this." When someone tells you to do something that is contrary to the teaching of God they are allowing the devil to have his way.

Remember, I said the Holy Spirit is more than a personification of good – the devil is more than a personification of evil. He has access to our minds. He is a spirit and he will get us to believe a lie any way he can. That is what happens when people leave their first love. That is what these Apostolic Age Christians did – they left their first love.

> 8. *And unto the angel of the church in Smyrna write; These things saith the first and the last, which was dead, and is alive;*
> 9. *I know thy works, and tribulation, and poverty, (but thou art rich) and I know the blasphemy of them which say they are Jews, and are not, but are the synagogue of Satan.*
> 10. *Fear none of those things which thou shalt suffer; behold the devil shall cast some of you into prison, that ye may be tried; and ye shall have tribulation ten days; be thou faithful unto death, and I will give thee a crown of life.*
> 11. *He that hath an ear, let him hear what the Spirit saith unto the churches; He that overcometh shall not be hurt of the second death.*

Jesus said, "Do not fear those who can kill the body."

Satan's followers were trying to stamp out Christianity in the world. It didn't work. It made the Christians more dedicated and brought them closer together.

I don't want to die a martyrs death, but if I have to, I know that it will mean, "to be absent from the body is to be at home with the Lord." You can't have anything better than that. Even though we do not want it, we may have to face this. Jesus says, *do not fear.*

He has no condemnation for this church age.

> 12. *And to the angel of the church in Pergamos write; These things saith he which hath the sharp sword with two edges;*

The angel, being the messenger, is the Holy Spirit of God. Otherwise, they would not have had the infallible message. God would not have charged a church that was receiving a fallible message. The people did not heed the infallible message, but the messenger would not override the will of the people.

13. *I know thy works, and where thou dwellest, even where Satan's seat is; and thou holdest fast my name, and hast not denied my faith, even in those days wherein Antipas was my faithful martyr, who was slain among you, where Satan dwelleth.*

Pergamos was the city known as the headquarters of Satan. Wherever there is effective teaching from the Word of God, Satan will be in the middle of it. He goes where the true Christian faith is being taught. Why would he want to go where he already has the people? This, also having an additional meaning, was a Church Age and we know from studying that the headquarters moved to Rome. Wouldn't Satan move wherever the effective teaching of God was being done? He is the enemy of God and the enemy of every Christian. He torments us continually by tempting us to sin and do wrong. He headquarters himself in the lives of everyone who wants to follow God and wants to believe what God has to say.

When the leaders of Rome decided that Christianity would be the State religion, pagan worship was stopped. The government officials were members of the church and they ruled paganism unlawful. The pagan buildings and statues were given to the church since the pagan worshippers were no longer allowed to use them. They chiseled off the pagan names, replaced them with Christian names, and the church, around A.D. 350, began owning real estate. The church went into the real estate business in the Pergama Age.

There is nothing wrong with having buildings to worship in, but there is something wrong with letting the building rule the church. The building is only a tool of worship. We must not allow a building to control us. Sometimes that happens. People say, "We paid for this building, we control it." I have been in churches across this State and I find ten to fifteen people sitting in nice big buildings with paved parking lots. I have a strong feeling this is what has happened. When people find out that a certain few control everything, it has a detrimental affect on the growth of the church.

...thou holdest fast my name,... This is a commendation. For the first time, during what I think is A.D. 312 through A.D. 606, the church was under governmental rule. Since the government leaders were also members of the church, they had what was known as the Nicene Council because there were differences of belief.

Nicolaitanism had already divided the people. They taught that the spiritual side of man was not responsible for what the physical side did. Then they decided that Christ could not possibly be the Divine Son of God, but that He was the best man that ever lived. Christ said, "I am the Son of God." Using logic, how can anyone say he is a liar, but he is the best man that ever lived? He cannot be both! He is either the Divine Son of God or He is a liar. This had to be settled in a meeting of the Nicene Council. Since it was a state church, Constantine, Emperor of Rome, chaired this meeting. One of the faithful men of God stood up and, according to church history, in order to prove the fact that he had suffered persecution for believing that Jesus Christ is the Divine Son of God, he took off his shirt and showed them his scars. There was a swell among the Council members. They were convinced that Jesus Christ was God in the flesh, that He was a God Man. This was a decision that came from the Council.

For many, many years Satan did not give them trouble. I think that is why we find here that Jesus said, *you hold fast my name.*

The liberal believers in this Council could not override the stronger spiritual believers. It was overwhelmingly decided that Jesus Christ was God in the flesh, that He existed before coming to this earth, and that He is as One with God. They had something in their favor. They did something good. They held fast His name. *...and hast not denied my faith,...* This was very important. They did not deny the faith. Some of these people were carryovers from the previous generation and that is why they had control in this Council. If the leaders of the Council were what they should have been, this question would never have been discussed.

14. *But I have a few things against thee, because thou hast there them that hold the doctrine of Balaam, who taught Balac to cast a stumbling block before the children of Israel, to eat things sacrificed unto idols, and to commit fornication.*
15. *So hast thou also them that hold the doctrine of the Nicolaitans, which thing I hate.*

This was happening toward the end of the Apostolic Church Age and here it is again. We cannot have false teaching mixed with Truth. A little bit of Truth with a lot of false teaching is worse than no Truth at all. This is how Satan works.

Here we have some ugly things showing up and these have caused many divisions in Christendom today. This was the headwater. They have spread all over the world... things that divide Christians.

Jesus said...*the doctrine of Balaam who taught Balac to cast a stumbling block before the children of Israel...* We find the account of Balaam in Numbers 22. He wanted God to give him a message to take to Balac and he wanted it to be something that would be victorious for him. God would not give him that message because it would be against the Israelite nation. Balaam refused to accept what God said. He wanted to have his way, so God said, "Go ahead and do it!" God does not supersede the will of man. We cannot understand it to mean that God approved, but He said, "Do it! If you are dead-set on doing it, do it! I am not going to supersede your will." I think that is what we find there. Balaam did what he wanted to do. He went to Balac and said: "If you want to bring down the Israelites put fleshly temptations in front of them." God did not approve of that. But Balaam did it even at the resistance of his mule. God allowed the animal to try to make Balaam reconsider. See how hard it is to change a person's mind once he or she has decided to do something? That is how "strong willed" people are. Sometimes they "will" themselves against God and that was what Balaam did. He put a stumbling block in front of the Israelite men. That stumbling block is being used today...not by this same false prophet, but by Satan's spiritual influence on people of every generation. What Balaam did was wrong. The Bible says he was a prophet of God at one time, but what he did in this incident was not approved of God. He was no longer a prophet when he disobeyed God.

Jesus still hates Nicolaitanism, but it has become an accepted teaching in the church today.

Nicola is a Greek word that, rightly translated, means to divide and conquer. This teaching caused some people to believe that the spiritual side of man was not responsible for what the physical side did. They said the acts of the flesh do not condemn us because "it's not my will that I sin." Oh how easy that is to say! I did not do it...my flesh did it.

This reminds me of our second daughter when she was about seven years old. She was having a disagreement with our youngest daughter. Before I could intervene, she hit her.

I was rather upset when she did that and I lashed out at her with my tongue. She just lowered her head, looked up, and said, "I didn't do it." I said, "I stood right here and watched you do it." She said, "My arm just flew out there." I could hardly keep from laughing, since our youngest daughter was not hurt too badly. It was not a good time for me to laugh, but... "My arm flew out there!" That is Nicolaitanism. It is the best way I know to explain what Nicola really is.

Satan is still using this teaching today to lure Christians into sin. In a discussion on this subject a friend told me, "There is no way a person who has become a Christian and has really been saved can be responsible for the deeds of the flesh." It is still being taught! I would like to accept that, but I cannot because it is not according to the Bible. We <u>are</u> <u>responsible</u> for the deeds of the flesh.

By teaching Nicolaitanism they were saying, "We will divide and call some of the people "laymen" and the other "clergy." The clergy will guide you in all Truth." That is one of Satan's lies. The Nicolaitan teaching of "divide and conquer" was building momentum.

The Word of God guides us in all Truth and is here for everyone to study. We are all fallible. We can only know the Truth as we find it in God's Word – spiritual Truth. If someone says they have miraculously received it another way then they are "like unto" the Nicolaitans. They are doing something to divide the church. We must not be guilty of dividing the church of the Lord Jesus Christ.

Martin Luther said, "Do not use my name or any other man's name to identify yourselves as Christians." He was a fallible man, but he did a lot of good.

16. Repent; or else I will come unto thee quickly, and will fight against them with the sword of my mouth.

36

There is nothing that people hate more, when they are living their lives contrary to the teaching of the Bible, than to have someone quote Scripture to them. I have had people get so mad at me that they probably wanted to hit me when I told them what the Bible says. They do not like to hear that. They say, "I've had a vision," or "I've had a dream," or "this strange thing happened to me." If it is not in the Word of God I do not accept it. My knowledge of the Bible was not revealed to me by some mysterious happening or dream, but by many hours of study.

There have always been people, though they may have been few, who have known and obeyed God's Word. I do not believe there has ever been a totally dark age. But we have a tendency to think things are getting so bad that perhaps there is no one left to preach the True gospel. Elijah thought he was the only one left, but God said, *"I have 7,000 people who have not bowed a knee to Baal."*

17. He that hath an ear, let him hear what the Spirit saith unto the churches; To him that overcometh will I give to eat of the hidden manna,

Have you heard this before? To him that overcomes, God will furnish heaven-supplied food. What is heaven-supplied food? It is the Holy Spirit breathed Word, the Word of God. He has the hidden manna for everyone who wants it. As the Israelites were able to eat every day and get the supply needed, we are able to go to the Word of God every day to get the supply we need to keep us, spiritually. I cannot go a day without spiritual food. If I do I am jeopardizing my spiritual life. I take the time every day to partake of the hidden manna, the heavenly food…we need to do that, as Christians. We cannot be a part of the royal priesthood if we are not partaking of the hidden manna.

*...and will give him a white stone, and in the stone a
new name written, which no man knoweth saving he that
receiveth it.*

The white stone signifies purity. White clothing has been
portrayed in the Bible as righteousness. The white stone
means pardoned of our sins, but does not mean that people
pay for their sins or that they deserve to be pardoned. We
are saved by grace...forgiven of our sins because of God's
grace. We who are willing to submit our lives to Him are
forgiven of our sins and receive a white stone.

18. *And unto the angel of the church in Thyatira write;
These things saith the Son of God, who hath his eyes
like unto a flame of fire, and his feet are like fine
brass;*

Notice, there is a difference in the way the churches are
addressed. Look at the church of Pergamos:

*...write; These things saith he which hath the sharp
sword with two edges, to the angel of the church.*

To both Church Ages the Son of God is identified, but
with a little different phrasing.

The Thyatira church did exist in that day. It no doubt
had characteristics of the description in Revelation, but we
cannot discount the fact that many prophecies and many
things in the Bible have more than one connection. One
reason I accept the thinking of the seven Church Ages is that
they can be so easily traced to exactly what the Bible says.

19. *I know thy works, and charity, and service, and faith,
and thy patience, and thy works; and the last to be
more than the first.*

We find here the Church Age of Thyatira (A.D. 606 – 1520) under tribulation. Jesus was not condemning this church. It was during this Church Age that the church established hospitals and did all kinds of charity work. They are not being put down for this. They are being highly exalted for their works, for their charity, service, faith, patience, works (again, as we find in that verse) and the last to be more than the first. He is saying that they had not diminished in this, but increased. Even today churches sponsor many of our hospitals. In the gospels, Jesus tells the Pharisees...these things ought you to have done and not have left the other things undone. I think that is what He is saying here. These works of charity, that are such a benefit to humanity, you ought to do, but you ought not to leave the others undone. What did they leave undone? They did not remain faithful to God!

The apostle John was the writer of the book of Revelation. John's style of writing in Revelation is different from his other writings. The only explanation I can give for this is that in the Gospel of John and First, Second and Third John, he was allowed a personality. He discounted his personality in Revelation and wrote exactly what was revealed to him. The apostle John was the recipient of the message from the Lord Jesus Christ. He was an old man at this time and the only one of the apostles that did not die a martyr's death.

> 20. *Notwithstanding I have a few things against thee, because thou sufferest that woman Jezebel, which calleth herself a prophetess, to teach and to seduce my servants to commit fornication, and to eat things sacrificed unto idols.*

They were allowing false prophets to teach in the church and lead people to believe that sin was actually approved. When you study church history, you will find that they paid for the right to indulge in sin. They had it pre-approved through the church. That is what Jesus meant when He said, *...you permit that woman Jezebel, which calleth herself a prophetess, to teach and to seduce my servants...*

They built hospitals, cathedrals – this was the richest Church Age, financially.

The Holy Spirit has revealed the message in Revelation for the full grown Christian. He did not reveal it for a casual reader of the Bible. It will mean more, as we dig and search for the Truth. Jesus said the gospel is like hidden treasure in a field. If a person knew that a field contained great wealth he would sell everything and buy the field. That is what we must do. You say, "Maybe a few people can do that, but not everyone." Christianity should be our main line, not our sideline. We should dig in the field constantly. We should think about the field constantly. We can work and do whatever we need to do, as far as the world is concerned, and still be turning those wheels about spiritual things. The Bible, God's Word, is the field with the treasure. It is not so well hidden that we cannot find it. It is there to be found, but it takes a diligent search.

One of the problems, in Christendom, has been the false idea that the only way you can take the gospel to the world is to win the whole world. You can take the gospel to the world and you can win a few people. But if you do not win them all it doesn't mean that you have not taken the gospel. The Bible is very clear that there will be more people lost than saved. One of my favorite men of the Old Testament is Noah. He preached the Word of God to everyone, but was only able to win his family. The Lord Jesus Christ recognizes him as a faithful preacher of righteousness. Noah understood that his only obligation was to tell the people God's Word, make it clear and plain, and let the people know he cared. Our job is to let people know that we care about them, that we want them to know the Truth.

The next verse lets us know that not only did the church exist in John's day, but it is a Church Age as well. When you look at the chart you will find that it was the longest Church Age and it produced what we know as the dark ages.

> *21. And I gave her space to repent of her fornication; and she repented not.*

Space – what is space? Space is time. Jesus Christ gave her space. This Church Age had from A.D. 606 to 1520 to repent and change. He said, *I gave her space to repent of her fornication and she repented not.*

It is very difficult for us, in this present Church Age, to identify with this. We have a tendency to think there were many denominations from the beginning of the church until now, but it was not that way. There were no denominations until after Martin Luther. Since then we have had branches of religion known by many and varied names.

> *22. Behold, I will cast her into a bed, and them that commit adultery with her into great tribulation, except they repent of their deeds.*

The church, being one at that time, was becoming saturated with false teaching. They sold everything they could to make money. They even sold the right to commit murder. The bigger the sin the more they charged. They were heading for trouble.

I will be talking later about tribulation that shall come upon all the earth. There are many places on the earth that have had tribulation throughout history. The tribulation mentioned in this verse is not one that covers the whole earth, but is associated with the church that is going in a direction contrary to God. He says they will run into trouble unless they repent.

23. And I will kill her children with death; and all the churches shall know that I am he which searcheth the reins and hearts; and I will give unto everyone of you according to your works.

Here we have a pronouncement of the punishment that is going to come.

As you study church history you will find a bloody battle going on within the ranks of the church during that period of time – toward the end of that age.

Jesus says, *And I will kill her children with death; and all the churches shall know that I am he which searcheth the reins and hearts:* How did He kill her children with death? The children mentioned here, who are members of this church, will die a spiritual death. Not physical death, but spiritual – they will die spiritually. People who are not faithful to God are flirting with spiritual death. We must remain faithful to God. The Bible does not say that we can do anything we want to do. The possibility of falling back into sin and being lost is not well accepted in Christendom today. You will not find many churches teaching this. When it is taught, it really knocks a hole in the belief that you can never be lost once you become a Christian (II Peter 3:20-22). God knows what we have in us. He knows what we think, what we believe, and how strong we believe it. We cannot hide from God.

...I will give unto every one of you according to your works.

Works – this is not a popular word in the church world. No one seems to like "works" – they like "grace." We must have both. Our faith will produce proof that we love God.

24. *But unto you I say, and unto the rest in Thyatira, as*
many as have not this doctrine, and which have not
known the depths of Satan, as they speak; I will put
upon you none other burden.
25. *But that which ye have already hold fast till I come.*
26. *And he that overcometh, and keepeth my works unto*
the end, to him will I give power over the nations:

As I have said, I do not believe there has ever been a total
eclipse of God's Word on this earth. I can prove that by this
book. Jesus says, "There are some here." When I think of
those people as I read verse 26: *And he that overcometh and*
*keepeth my works unto the end...*it tells me there was a small
flicker of light. Satan was very successful in <u>almost</u> putting
out the light of the church and this was called the Dark Ages.
He was not able to put it out completely. There was still a
flicker of light.

27. *And he shall rule them with a rod of iron; as the*
vessels of a potter shall they be broken to shivers;
even as I received of my Father.

As I look at this, I see the torchbearers. As we have seen
on television, someone carries a torch so far and then passes
it on to someone else and he or she to someone else. The
people who are bearing the torch are people who are making
identity with whatever event it may be. They are carrying the
torch as a symbol of this.

The torchbearers of that Age carried the Word of God
to the next Age. Jesus said, *I will give them power over the*
nations.

As the gospel came forth we find men who had enough
courage to stand up for the Truth.

In Wittenberg, Germany, Martin Luther named ninety-
five things that the church was doing wrong, according to the

Commentary On The Revelation Of Jesus Christ

Bible. He became a torchbearer for the Truth of the Word. There have been many others that have been torchbearers for the Truth.

As we look at the world today, hasn't it broken into pieces? The false teaching that was controlled by a one-world church, that was made a political power, as well as a false prophet power in the world, has been exposed. They have acknowledged it.

28. And I will give him the morning star.
29. He that hath an ear, let him hear what the Spirit saith unto the churches.

...I will give him the morning star. This is a first blessing.

Did you ever go out in the very early morning? Years ago we milked cows by hand. I remember walking out, looking up at the sky, and seeing the morning star. It gave more light than anything else at that time; it was actually lighting up the sky.

This star mentioned in the twenty eighth verse is still giving Light today. Those faithful few may be why we are worshipping God today. It can continue to shine if we hold to the Truth of God's Word. He has a lot of good things in store for those who love Him.

He that hath an ear, let him hear... We can listen to something and not hear it. We must listen and hear! When we hear it we have taken it in and digested it. The spiritual side of our life is fed from God's Word. We like to feed our physical bodies with physical food. Let's develop the same desire to feed the spiritual side of our life with spiritual food. Then we will have complete satisfaction. My heart aches for people who do not partake of the spiritual food. I see them having physical satisfaction, but I see that they are just half there. I would love to be able to say, "Here, take some spiritual nourishment." But it's a little more difficult than that. They will not partake unless they truly want to know God's Word.

CHAPTER 3

1. And unto the angel of the church in Sardis write; These things saith he that hath the seven Spirits of God, and the seven stars; I know thy works, that thou hast a name that thou livest, and art dead.

In addition to the church in John's day I believe there was a Church Age that we can identify as well. Since it is in the past we are not speculating and saying something that is not true or cannot be proven. When we trace church history we can find what this Church Age produced. Why did they have a name that lived, but they were dead? They depended, totally, upon works. As we studied the last Church Age, we saw that their works were so great; their charity was something that increased.

We find in the Bible what sin is and we also find doctrinal teaching. It was revealed to us of the Holy Spirit through the apostles and those they chose to lay their hands upon.

Without the doctrinal practices they appeared to be living, but they were dead. Here we have the grimmest Church Age in the history of the world. It was from A.D. 1520 to 1776.

Martin Luther's background in the Roman Church influenced his mode of worship. For instance, infant baptism – he didn't see anything wrong with that at all. I will talk more about infant baptism later.

I believe we are now branching from what was identified as the Roman Church. We will be dealing with a mainstream religion that is closer to the Word of God as we continue on through the Church Ages in our study.

> 2. *Be watchful, and strengthen the things which remain, that are ready to die; for I have not found thy works perfect before God.*
> 3. *Remember therefore how thou hast received and heard, and hold fast, and repent. If therefore thou shalt not watch, I will come on thee as a thief, and thou shalt not know what hour I will come upon thee.*

The people of this Church Age felt good about themselves. They were confident that they had the approval of God. At the final judgment when the Lord pronounces their condemnation it will come as a thief...a total surprise.

The Sardis Church Age, that was dead spiritually, did not know what God had told them. These people were not only to remember what was identified as sin, but they were to also remember where the message came from. That is what the Holy Spirit is saying here...remember how and where you have received the Truth. We must remember where it comes from.

The thinking of every Christian in the royal priesthood should be, "We are watchmen over one another." Every shepherd is a sheep and every sheep is a shepherd. This is a slogan we should never forget. This is the way God set it up. We are to be guardians of one another when it comes to teaching the scriptures.

Jesus said remember where you found the Truth...in the Bible, the Word of God. There we can settle all arguments, disputes, or debates for the honest-hearted Christian.

We are saved by grace and not by our works. But remember that God has direction for us. It is called doctrine.

It is very important to be accurate where God's Word is concerned.

In the Old Testament of the Bible, our schoolmaster, God is letting us see what happened to the people who did not obey Him. God says do what I say. He punished those people of the Old Testament for not doing what He said. In this New Testament dispensation, if we do not obey what God tells us in His Word, we will receive our punishment at the final judgment.

> *4. Thou hast a few names even in Sardis which have not defiled their garments; and they shall walk with me in white: for they are worthy.*

Even during this Church Age there were a few names... those that had remained faithful. This means there was a glimmer of Light that did not go out. There was a Dark Age, but not totally.

...and they shall walk with me in white:... We put on the righteousness of Christ, not our own. I think we have a misconception in the world about this. Our obedience to the Lord in all things is counted to us as righteousness.

The Sardis Church Age resulted in a "back to the Bible" study and it made the Word of God available to the people once again. The Word of God had been taken from the "layman." The church leaders of that day said, "You cannot understand it, so why read it? Let us interpret it for you." Luther's movement did encourage a back to the Bible study, and this produced faithful Christians.

> *5. He that overcometh, the same shall be clothed in white raiment and I will not blot out his name out of the book of life, but I will confess his name before my Father, and before his angels.*

6. He that hath an ear, let him hear what the Spirit saith unto the churches.

Hold fast (in verse 3) means to accept only the doctrine clearly taught in the Scriptures. We also have the word *repent* in that verse. Those who repented will walk with the Lord in white.

In the fifth verse we find the book of life mentioned. This is a puzzling thing to many people in the world today. I have a couple of questions on it:

- How do I get in the book of life?
- How am I blotted out of the book of life?

These are two things we must think about because we find a lot about the book of life in the Bible. In the Old Testament scriptures God said, *When you were in your mother's womb, I knew you.* So I cannot say that we go into the book of life when we are born, but when we are conceived.

As I thought about this I felt I must put in a few words of anti-abortion teaching here. I thought, "When the apostle Paul faces Stephen in heaven I'm sure it will be with open arms." Paul helped murder Stephen, but later repented of what he had done and was forgiven. I have no doubt at all that they both will be in heaven. A mother who has aborted her child may meet that child in heaven. Think about it a little bit. There will be mothers in heaven who will have aborted their children and the children will be there.

Back to the book of life...it is possible for everyone, upon being conceived, to remain there during his or her entire life. If a person becomes a Christian and remains faithful to God's Word, he or she will never go off the book of life. We cannot defend our position against infant baptism without this teaching. The purpose of infant baptism is to put the baby in the book of life – only then can they be saved.

This is the theology and doctrine of infant baptism. We can only defend our position by declaring that they are on the book of life when they are conceived. When they reach the age of accountability they become chargeable for their sins. Anyone who is not of sound mind or not accountable to make decisions will stay on it. But anyone who is of sound mind and able to make decisions, is able to discern the gospel plan of salvation, but refuses to accept it, will be blotted out when they die. In other words, if a person goes through life without ever acknowledging Christ as Savior then his or her name will be blotted out of the book of life. A person who has once known Christ as Savior, but has grown cold and indifferent toward the Holy Spirit revealed message, will be blotted out. These scriptures verify this: II Peter 2:20, 21; Hebrews 10:26; Jude, verses 5 and 6; and I John 5:16-17. Three reasons for being blotted out of the book of life are:

- Dying after living a life without accepting Christ – his/her name will be blotted out at death.
- Becoming cold and indifferent toward the revealed Word of the Holy Spirit, after once knowing Christ as Savior – his/her name will be blotted out at death.
- Taking away from the words of the book of this prophecy (Revelation 22:19) will result in a name being blotted out of the book of life.

We are sure of heaven if we die before we reach the age of accountability or if we are unable to be responsible in our thinking.

We have a level of exposure that is just like an educational process. It comes to some earlier than others. I think the adult is responsible to God for accepting a young person's profession of faith. We are doing wrong to reject a child simply due to age. It really makes me angry when someone refuses to accept the profession of faith from a seven, eight, nine or ten year old child because of their age. That is not right.

The next church is a pleasant church to talk about. It is one that our Lord counted very effective and He praised it highly. There is very little written concerning this church history.

I have a book entitled Historical Documents Advocating Christian Union, by C. A. Young. There was a reprint of this book by College Press in 1985. It is no longer in print or available. It is a very important book to me. We should try to get another reprint of this and get it into the hands of the people. There is some very important history in this book. It is the only document on record that I have found which covers the Restoration Movement and what I think is the Philadelphian Church Age. This Church Age started in the late 1700's and I am happy to say continues today. I am not trying to sell a book because it is not for sale. You cannot find it. When the Bible was taken out of the hands of the people we had a Dark Age. If we take these kind of enlightening facts from the hands of the people we are headed for another Dark Age.

At one time there was a resentment of the Restoration Movement in the denominational world. When Campbell rightly divided the Word of Truth, the Redstone Baptist Association tried him for being a heretic. He said, "I won by three votes from three kind individuals who only voted for me because they liked me." But they eventually expelled him. Can you believe he was expelled for teaching that there is a division between the Old and New Testament? It is all recorded in the book called Historical Documents.

7. *And to the angel of the church in Philadelphia write;...*

The word Philadelphia means brotherly love. Isn't that coincidental? The Philadelphia church did exist in John's day. It was established during the apostles' day. Another astounding thing about this church of Philadelphia was the fact that it remained an independent Christian church for 1400 years. They were plagued with earthquakes and various things of this nature. The Turks eventually over ran them and, of course, that was the end of the city of Philadelphia. But it stood longer than any other city mentioned where an independent Christian church had been established. That says a lot.

...These things saith he that is holy, he that is true, he that hath the key of David, he that openeth, and no man shutteth; and shutteth, and no man openeth;

...the key of David... Jesus Christ was of the lineage of David. David was promised that his throne would be established forever, that someone connected with him and his family would reign forever, and that it would be an everlasting kingdom. We have the reiteration of this fact in this book of prophecy. He that hath the key of David is none other than Jesus Christ, the Lion of the tribe of Judah. Our Lord Jesus Christ died for the church. He created the church. We say that He created it because anything that is not created evolves from something before it. Nothing of its likeness preceded it. We might say, "What about the Old Testament scripture and all that leads up to the church?" It did lead up to it and there was a promise of One coming. This promise was fulfilled in Jesus Christ. His coming also fulfilled the prophecy concerning David. Jesus Christ is a descendant of David and *...he hath the key of David.* His coming had already been announced.

Jesus made it very clear in the parable of the wineskins that He was not revamping an old system. He said you do not put new wine in old bottles, but you put new wine in new bottles, or skins.

Grape juice was preserved in skins. When they had a new skin, it was cured and made ready for filling. It was filled, sealed, and dropped in water. The contents remained as fresh as the day it was put in.

The teaching in this parable is...if you put new wine in old wineskins it will not be preserved. Jesus then connects this with the church, which tells us that He was not revamping an old system, that He was not bringing an old system over, but that He was creating a new system. Therefore, we have the Old Testament as a schoolmaster. The church, established on the Day of Pentecost, is not something that has evolved from Judaism. This is what Jesus is saying.

It is a church of the open door. ...*he that openeth, and no man shutteth; and shutteth, and no man openeth*; He opened the door to the royal priesthood. What does this royal priesthood mean to us? The entire royal priesthood of believers can evangelize, teach, and baptize. It means that we can go to God in prayer, that we can study from His Holy Word, and that we can win people to the Lord Jesus Christ, according to the Bible. This is what the Bible teaches. The only test for a minister of the gospel is – do you know the Word? Will you stick to the Word? Will you change if you find that you are wrong, according to the Word? The Word of God has made a big difference in a person's life that was willing to change. The reward is great for those who are faithful to God. The open door – the whole priesthood of believers has the same opportunity to study and to know God's Word.

8. *I know thy works: behold, I have set before thee an open door, and no man can shut it: for thou hast a little strength, and hast kept my word, and hast not denied my name.*

He says I know your works and I have set before you an open door. The open door, of course, is the fact that the gospel is free to go forth into the world...to every person that lives on the earth.

Just last week I heard a comment on television: "If they want religion let them have it in their own church buildings." That is the work of Satan. He is working through the governments of the world trying to shut the door on evangelism.

God says, *you are a small number*, when He speaks of the people who are trying to do what the Bible teaches and who are speaking where the Bible speaks. He says, *you have little strength, but you have kept my Word.* It is important with God to keep His Word. We cannot glorify Him by inventing our own religion. We can only glorify God by following His plan of salvation, His Word.

> *9. Behold, I will make them of the synagogue of Satan, which say they are Jews, and are not, but do lie; behold, I will make them to come and worship before thy feet, and to know that I have loved thee.*

The false teachers will one day acknowledge the Bible as the only Truth. Someone may say, "A mysterious thing happened to me and I believe it was from God." If it cannot be proven in the scriptures then it is not of God. It cannot be counted for doctrine, for instruction, for reproof, and correction because it does not stand the test. People who say they have the truth, but do not have it according to the word of God will one day have to acknowledge that the Word of God was, is, and will be, the only Truth. That is why He says, *...which say they are Jews, and are not, but do lie.*

> *10. Because thou hast kept the word of my patience, I also will keep thee from the hour of temptation, which*

shall come upon all the world, to try them that dwell upon the earth.

This group, though small in number, will be lifted from the earth and the rest of the world will know little about what has happened.

I think the world will be ready for a "one religious system." It will be ready for a "one governmental system" and it will take over at this point in time. When the disappearance of true Christians from the earth takes place, some of the people that are left will try to explain it away. The one world religious system will say it was not the lifting of Christians from the earth.

Read I Thessalonians 4:17. Do not make the mistake of breaking the thought at the end of Chapter 4. Read the first verse of the fifth chapter where Paul says "times." Some translations say "times and seasons" and others say "times and dates." In the original text both are plural which sheds a lot of light. Those who say that it will all happen at one time and one date – where are they getting the idea? The devil has his way sometimes with the minds of translators in dividing chapters.

I Thessalonians 4:16 through 5:1

For the Lord himself shall descend from heaven with a shout, with the voice of the archangel, and with the trump of God: and the dead in Christ shall rise first:

Then we which are alive and remain shall be caught up together with them in the clouds, to meet the Lord in the air: and so shall we ever be with the Lord. Wherefore comfort one another with these words:

We know this is not the end of this chapter because it says,

But of the times and the seasons, brethren, ye have no need that I write unto you.

We have a tendency to stop at the end of one chapter and start another thought at the beginning of the next chapter.

This will include the Old and New Testament saints, the 144,000 first fruits (first converts) mentioned in Revelation 14:4.

...I also will keep thee from the hour of temptation...

No other Church Age has been promised that they will be kept from this hour of temptation. As we look at this Church Age we realize the only thing that can possibly take place is that God will lift them from the earth just before the hour of *trial* (NIV), *which shall come upon all the world.* When we talk about trials on the earth we think of things happening in one or two locations, but not *upon all the world.*

11. *Behold, I come quickly: hold that fast which thou hast, that no man take thy crown.*
12. *Him that overcometh will I make a pillar in the temple of my God, and he shall go no more out: and I will write upon him the name of my God, and the name of the city of my God, which is new Jerusalem, which cometh down out of heaven from my God: and I will write upon him my new name.*
13. *He that hath an ear, let him hear what the Spirit saith unto the churches.*

The disappearance of true believers will be an awakening. The people left, who are of a spiritual nature, will be seeking spiritual Truth. They will realize the false teachers have told them things that are not true.

As with all Church Ages, one overlaps the other. This Philadelphian Age has overlapped into the Laodicean Age and it will be small in number. The Laodicean Church Age will go into the tribulation period.

As I have said before, God is in the soul saving business. He is not out to condemn or destroy. If God was only thinking about destroying the people on earth He could have done that in the beginning and still remained a just God. He wants to save those who are willing to change and look to Him.

Jesus commissioned the church to go, in Matthew 28:19. Here He announces "mission accomplished" to the Philadelphian Church Age. And you shall go out no more – thanks, I now present to you your eternal gift. Your new identity – transfer from mortal to immortality in the twinkling of an eye.

According to the World Book Encyclopedia and other historical documents John Paul the Twenty-Third was chosen as Pope in 1958 (58 – 63). The first thing he did was call for a meeting with the Roman Diocese. He had an urgent agenda. It was to reform Canon Law. A change was declared and he announced it to the world. He said that all denominations were children of the mother church and that regardless of doctrinal teaching should evangelize the world as one. This was the beginning of the Laodicean Lukewarm Age in the denominational world. If we look around today we find that everything in the religious world is leaning in that direction. It seems to be the only thing that will satisfy people. They will accept anyone's belief.

In the 1970's I remember reading in our Standard material about something called Key 74. There was going to be a new evangelistic approach to the world. It would involve all denominations and all "Christ centered" religions. They may not be Biblically correct, but if they are Christ centered, they felt, this would be sufficient. Here we find the beginning, in the Christian church, of the Laodicean Lukewarm Age.

Some of our ministers readily accept an invitation to preach a revival or dedication day message in any denominational congregation without telling them there is a specific Bible doctrine to be believed. I think by doing so, it is a disservice to the people they are speaking to. It is also telling the world that it does not make any difference what you believe. If we love these people and care for them, the first thing we should do, if they ask us to speak, is tell them and correct them in what we know they are not following according to the Word of God.

"Our religious training schools are claiming the spiritual oversight of local congregations." One of our professors made this statement at the First Christian Church, Radcliff, Kentucky in 1975. I was present and I made a note of it. The Bible does not say that our religious training schools are spiritual overseers, but that the elders are the spiritual overseers for each congregation. When this is removed from the eldership then we are susceptible to any change the training institutions want to make.

A man should never be ordained without being fully trained and qualified for the eldership. The evangelist has this duty and responsibility. It is also important for us to realize that when there are unqualified elders in the church it is not all the evangelists' fault. It could be the present eldership and the fact that they are not making sure the necessary training is available for qualifying men as elders and deacons. That is happening in our Christian congregations.

The Restoration Movement, which had such an impact in the world, was to restore Bible teaching in the church and that has all but vanished. Some people say quit "piddling around" with studying the Bible – get out and convert the world. I say we had better not think Bible study is killing time.

Let me bring to your attention some Bible that is from the schoolmaster. Moses, in the Old Testament scripture, failed to do something that might be considered a waste of time. God was going to let him die for not doing it. His wife did not want him to circumcise their son. Moses became ill and was on his deathbed. Zipporah knew why he was sick and she knew why he was going to die. She circumcised their son and threw the skin at Moses' feet (Exodus 4:24-26). God requires precise obedience to His Word and He does not accept anything else.

God told Achan to not take spoils from the war. But the things looked good and were very useful, so he took what he wanted and hid it. The whole nation suffered because he disobeyed God.

If we do not know the Old Testament we cannot understand the New Testament.

I told you that the faithful Christians are lifted from the earth. The people who have such a broad spectrum that they feel they are Christ-centered even though they are not Bible based, will go into the trials that shall be upon all the earth.

We must be knowledgeable of the spiritual things that are going on in the world. We cannot put our head into the sand and say we do not care what people do when it comes to spiritual matters. If I do not know and I can know, then I will be held responsible just the same.

It took me two years to figure out that the back-sliden Laodicean Church Age that goes into the tribulation period is sandwiched in between the third and fourth chapter. In chronological order, when we finish with the Philadelphia Church we can easily go into the fourth chapter of the book of Revelation and read: *After this I looked and behold a door was open in heaven.* That is what happens at the end of the Philadelphia Church Age that overlaps into the Laodicean Age. Let me bring something to your attention that is not unusual. Have you ever watched a movie where they show a scene in the middle or show a scene near the end? It is not unusual at all. It took me so long to get this and get it in perspective. The faithful, Bible believing Christians of the

Philadelphian Church Age are lifted seven years before the
end of the Laodicean Age (remember – they overlap).

I will go on through and teach it in the order it is written
in the Bible.

> *14. And unto the angel of the church of the Laodiceans
> write; These things saith the Amen, the faithful and
> true witness, the beginning of the creation of God;*
> *15. I know thy works, that thou art neither cold nor hot:
> I would thou wert cold or hot.*

There is a marvelous amount of information here.

I am going to give you some fiction. Where I live, the
water froze at 40 degrees this morning. You don't believe
that do you? I don't believe it because it did not happen. We
know that it has to be 32 degrees before water will freeze. At
our sea level, at what temperature does water boil? It has to
be 212 degrees.

If I were to ask every one of you, me included, to go out
and get a cup of lukewarm water I guarantee you there will
not be two of them the same temperature. But what will it
be? It will be the temperature that you decide is lukewarm.

Marvin Hornback wanted me to get him a cup of coffee
one night as we were coming back from a "Men for Christ"
meeting. I said, "Sure, I will." I got two cups of coffee –
one for each of us. He took the top off his cup and drank
about half of it. I said, "Do you have any mouth left?" I was
half way home before I could take a drink of mine. He said,
"Well, it's just warm to me."

Do you see what I mean? Everyone's lukewarm is his or
her own decision.

What are we talking about when we speak of being lukewarm in religion? What is it? It is whatever you decide is
right – whatever I decide is right.

Jesus is saying that in lukewarm religion there are no absolutes. In the Bible there are definitely absolutes. There is Truth in the Bible to be pursued. There is a right and a wrong. Our God is not a wishy-washy God. He hates lukewarm when it comes to our obedience to Him. He said, *I would that you were either cold or hot.*

This is a Church Age that has decided on its own religious beliefs and has made its own rules.

I heard a television evangelist make a statement last week. He said, "We have all kinds of different denominations in the world. They all have different teachings and different beliefs. We need to ignore correction because we are not that far apart anyway."

We are in it my friends! We are in the Laodicean Church Age.

16. *So then because thou art lukewarm, and neither cold nor hot, I will spue thee out of my mouth.*

17. *Because thou sayest, I am rich, and increased with goods, and have need of nothing; and knowest not that thou art wretched, and miserable, and poor, and blind, and naked:*

You say you are rich, you know everything, you can decide on your own religion. You say you do not need anything. Know you not that you are miserable, poor, blind, and naked?

Without the righteousness of God we have no clothing – we have absolutely nothing.

18. *I counsel thee to buy of me gold tried in the fire, that thou mayest be rich; and white raiment, that thou mayest be clothed, and that the shame of thy nakedness do not appear; and anoint thine eyes with eyesalve, that thou mayest see.*

He is appealing to the individual. Notice what He is doing. He is not going to the leadership. He is not going to the heads of the organizations because they are already so deep in this theory that they will not be turned around. God is still interested in individuals, but He does not supersede our will. He is appealing to individuals now to "Come to me that you may be rich and wear white raiment for clothing to cover yourselves."

How do we go to God? We go on His terms. We go to God through His Word and the direction He has given there. We take the directions He has given, apply them to our lives, and this becomes clothing for us.

I will not have anything to brag about when I reach the eternal shores. I will just thank God for forgiveness, direction, and the gold that has been tried in the fire. His Word is gold tried in the fire. If you think it isn't, just study the Church Ages and see the many deaths from all kinds of cruelty to Christians.

19. As many as I love, I rebuke and chasten: be zealous therefore, and repent.

Who does God love? Let's look at this for a minute. Clear away the things that are causing you not to understand and accept My Word. Jesus is saying this in the eighteenth and nineteenth verse. Get everything out of your mind that is standing in the way of you accepting My Word and taking My directions.

God says He loved us before we ever loved Him in return. He loved us so much that He sent His only Son to die for us.

Keeping the commandments of God, by those who have acknowledged Him as Lord and Savior, is very important to Him. He will teach and guide in all Truth in His Holy Word.

We have to be careful with our interpretation of this word "chasten." If you make a careful study of the word, you will find that it means discipline – spiritual teaching.

Sometimes things happen to us that can work together for good if we love God. As these things are working together for good for those who love Him, this is God allowing us to use the misery of the sin curse to draw closer to Him. It is an over-powering of Satan through strength that can only come from God. He is showing how the sin curse and the misery that Satan has brought upon this world can be turned around. We have no escape except the arms of God. God is more powerful than Satan. The sin curse affects everyone, even the animals, and the earth we are living on. God did not do it – Satan did it. God is more powerful and He can use it.

A man told me that God had called him to be a preacher. He was the worst alcoholic in the paint section where I worked. One day I said, "Larry, I understand that you feel you were called to preach." He said, "I was." I said, "I'm sure you do not deny that you have an alcohol problem. We can all see that here at work. You are a good guy and a good friend, but you have an alcohol problem that is actually killing you." He said, "I know it, but when God gets ready for me to stop, He will stop me." I thought, "Then you believe you are drinking because God is making you drink." No, God was not making him drink. He was drinking because he refused to discipline himself. God chastens us through His Word. It is our fault that we sin, not God's fault. I could never get him to understand this. The man died a few years ago. It was a premature death because of his drinking. He must have died a very confused man. I am sorry about that. My life touched his, but I could not change him because of tradition he had been taught.

A belief such as this is why I say that one of the things dividing the church today is tradition. We are chastened and disciplined by God when we study His Word and apply it to our lives.

Ephesians 4:4-6
> 4. *There is one body, and one Spirit, even as ye are called in one hope of your calling;*
> 5. *One Lord, one faith, one baptism,*
> 6. *One God and Father of all, who is above all, and through all, and in you all.*

One Lord, one faith, one baptism – this is important for us to remember. In fact, remembering this scripture is so important it could determine whether we escape the great tribulation.

> 20. *Behold, I stand at the door, and knock: if any man hear my voice, and open the door, I will come in to him, and will sup with him, and he with me.*

Notice that Jesus placed himself on the outside of our heart's door. What He is saying is that He will not supersede our will, but He will be waiting. He said, "I stand at your heart's door and knock." In other words, "I am anxiously waiting for you to let me in – for you to recognize where your security is." All we have to do is open the door. All we have to do is make the decision – intelligently decide. That is what the prodigal son did. He said, "I am out here feeding animals that we Jews will not even eat. I am eating the same food that I feed the swine. How low can I get! I remember my father." That is what we need to do – remember our Father. Jesus said, "I'm waiting, I'm standing at the door." The prodigal son only had to say, "I know my father will receive me; I need to go to him." That is what we need to do with God. That is what the Laodicean Church Age needs to do – return to God. Open the door to Him and He will come in. The latch is on the inside – on our side.

Verse 21 is an appeal to individuals. We can each be personally acquainted with God. In other words, we do not have to be a mass of people. He appeals to individuals here through their study of the Word, even though the Laodicean Church Age is vast and so controlled by the hierarchy of the church.

Remember these things: The Christians will be lifted off the earth prior to the end of the Laodicean Church Age. This scripture (14-22) is a brief summary of the spiritual condition of the Laodicean Church.

I can show you as I continue to teach through Revelation that there will be more people saved from the Laodicean Church Age. They will remember every person that disappears. They will say, "I knew them, I knew what they stood for, I remember what they said." There is never going to be a more repentant and/or zealous people than these. I will prove it to you by the Bible.

The lack of study, of the book of Revelation, has gotten us into trouble in the church and I hate that.

21. To him that overcometh will I grant to sit with me in my throne, even as I also overcame, and am set down with my Father in His throne.

What kind of throne does Jesus have and what is He talking about here when He says you can sit with me in My throne? He did not say sit with Me as the Divine Son of God. We are not to be worshipped, so what did Jesus mean when He said, *To him that overcometh will I grant to sit with me in my throne?* What kind of throne does He have that is different from the one where He sits at the right hand of God? He makes intercession for us. We will not make intercession for anyone, so we have to eliminate that. When I eliminate everything these people cannot do, then I have to say, "What will some people in the Laodicean Church Age do that will give them the right to sit in the throne of Jesus Christ?" They will be martyred! The martyrs throne! Jesus was martyred. He was slain. This is what will happen to these people. I will point it out to you later. They are going to be slain because they do not take the mark of the beast. Brothers and sisters we may be gone...I hope we are. I hope we are lifted off the earth before this happens. The people of the Laodecian Church Age, that begin to recognize the importance of God's Word, will see the Oneness of the Father, Son, and Holy Spirit. When they do not take the mark of the beast Satan will have the power to put them to death. There will be mass killings of the people that turn to God from this Church Age. These people will share the martyrs throne with the Lord. I do not want you to share that throne and I don't want to share it either.

22. *He that hath an ear, let him hear what the Spirit saith unto the churches.*

I said earlier that I felt the Restoration Movement has been a great blessing to the world. I do not want to impress upon you that I think the only people lifted from the earth will be people identified with the Christian Church, Restoration Movement, or Church of Christ. This may raise a question in your mind. You may say, "How can you think otherwise?" I will tell you what I mean.

Yesterday morning when I was working in my yard, a man stopped by. As we began to talk, we got on the subject of Christianity. This man was not a member of the Christian Church, but he said he believes the Bible is the only rule we can go by.

These people are scattered – they are scattered all over the world. I do not believe that everyone who is a member of the Christian Church will be a part of the lifting of Christians from the earth.

I have never believed that any group of people or any individual has a monopoly on the Bible. The world is free to study the Bible and to know it because of the royal priesthood. So therefore, we cannot make dogmatic statements about people that we do not know. I have met many people in this world that love God, love His Word, and do not want anything else but His Word.

I told you that we are still in the Philadelphian Church Age and that the Laodicean Church Age has already started.

Jesus says, (chapter 3:11) *Behold, I come quickly: hold that fast which thou hast, that no man take thy crown.* This is at the consummation of the Philadelphian Church Age. I do not know when this will happen. The apostle Paul did not know. Jesus did not tell us.

I think, from my study, that the Philadelphian Church Age has been here since the 1700's. Great revivals began to take place throughout the world and people wanted to return to the Bible. This was a fulfillment of what the Bible says about the Philadelphian Church Age.

The Holy Spirit tells us that the back-sliden Laodicean Church Age will go into the tribulation period. Jesus says that some people will be saved from this group. Every person that does not take the mark of the beast and become subject to a one-world church, one world government, and one world financial system, will be killed.

Immediately after Jesus says, *Behold, I come quickly* (through verse 13) to the Philadelphian Church Age, we go to the fourth chapter. The Laodicean Church Age is talked about (3:14-22) between the calling forth of the true believers from the earth in the Philadelphian Church Age and what we are about to see here.

CHAPTER 4

1. After this I looked, and, behold, a door was opened in heaven: and the first voice which I heard was as it were of a trumpet talking with me; which said, Come up hither, and I will shew thee things which must be hereafter.

We now have a scene in heaven as Jesus says to John, "I want to show you all the things which must be hereafter."

2. And immediately I was in the spirit: and, behold, a throne was set in heaven, and one sat on the throne.

John is transferred from earth to heaven. He sees one throne. Jesus Christ has said, "*All power is given unto me in heaven and in earth*" *Matthew 28:18*. Jesus is sitting on the throne in heaven.

We need to recognize that Jesus rescued mankind from earth. We must worship Him out of gratitude and love for what He has done for us. He did something for us that no one else could do. He became flesh and blood, subject to the limitations of a human being. He put those limitations on Himself in order that He might go to the cross, suffer, bleed, and die, for our sins.

There is a throne set in heaven and the One who holds the seat of authority is our High Priest, Jesus Christ.

> *3. And he that sat was to look upon like a jasper and a sardine stone: and there was a rainbow round about the throne, in sight like unto an emerald.*

The High Priest in the Old Testament had twelve stones set in his garment. Each of these twelve stones represented one of the twelve tribes. The Israelite people knew exactly which stone represented each tribe. The first stone mentioned in this verse and the last one mentioned is the first and the last stone in the breastplate of the High Priest of the Old Testament. This signifies that not only the saints of the church era, but also those of the Old Testament era will come under the blood of Christ. The Old Testament saints had to believe God's promise that by the seed of a woman He would bruise the head of Satan and that this was prophecy of the coming of Christ. Believing this would bring them under His blood.

In the third verse we have a scene regarding the One sitting on the throne and His appearance. It says there was a rainbow round about the throne.

Have you noticed that we only see a part of the rainbow? The rainbow always reminds us of God's promise that He will never again destroy the world with water.

The rainbow mentioned in this verse will be round about the throne and will be a perfect circle without end.

When we perform weddings we take the little band of gold and say that it is a perfect circle. Being a circle, it is without end and we are hoping that this uniting together will be without end as well.

The *rainbow round about the throne* signifies a relationship with God where all tears will be wiped away. All suffering, all hunger, all pain, all the things that beset us here on earth will no longer exist. This perfect state will never end.

> *4. And round about the throne were four and twenty seats: and upon the seats I saw four and twenty elders sitting, clothed in white raiment; and they had on their heads crowns of gold.*

...round about the throne were four and twenty seats: This reminds us of the Old Testament and the twenty-four priests that represented the entire priesthood. As we look at the Patriarchal and Mosaical dispensations of the Old Testament we find that there was a head of each of the twelve tribes. We see in the New Testament era of time that there were twelve apostles. These combined make twenty-four. Just as those twenty-four priests in the Old Testament represented all of the Levitical priesthood, these twenty-four seats represent the Patriarchal, Mosaical, and Christian dispensations. They are called elders. *...clothed in white raiment*, means they are washed in the blood of Jesus Christ and made white as snow, just as we are. If they could be identified as any other beings from the Bible or as heavenly beings it would not be significant that they are dressed in white robes. The fact that they are dressed in white robes leads us to believe they are redeemed from the earth – redeemed by the blood of Jesus Christ. They have crowns of gold. They accomplished the job they had to do.

> *5. And out of the throne proceeded lightnings and thunderings and voices: and there were seven lamps of fire burning before the throne, which are the seven Spirits of God.*

There are seven spirits of God, which are identified as activities of the Holy Spirit and His power.

The lightnings, thunderings, and voices are telling us that judgment is about to take place on the earth.

From the time of the lifting from the earth of the resurrected Old Testament saints, the resurrected Church Age saints, and the transformation of the living, until the end of the great tribulation, will be seven years.

After the disappearance of Christians from the earth, these lukewarm, back-sliden Laodicean Church Age people will be searching the Bible.

God will do everything He can do without superseding their will. During this seven years God will press them for a decision. Someone said to me, "That cannot be because it will give the people a second chance." I said, "How many chances have you had?" He didn't say. I am glad that I have had more than one. If God presses for a decision from the people left on earth to save them, He will not have a problem from me.

> 6. *And before the throne there was a sea of glass like unto crystal: and in the midst of the throne, and round about the throne, were four beasts full of eyes before and behind.*

Before the throne is a sea of glass. The Bible makes reference to the sea as people. This indicates the masses of people. Being *a sea of glass* tells us that it is not troubled, but calm. The people standing round about are calm, content and happy. It is a still sea, like glass. When we see a body of water that is like glass, we say there is no wind, no trouble on the water. There definitely will not be trouble there because the people will be with God.

...round about the throne were four beasts full of eyes before and behind. These are personnel of God in heaven.

> *7. And the first beast was like a lion, and the second beast was like a calf, and the third beast had a face as a man, and the fourth beast was like a flying eagle.*

They are called beasts because they are powerful. They have eyes that they can see in any direction, so there is no hiding from them. They have been longing and waiting for the sin curse to be lifted. It has caused suffering for every living thing on the earth...wild animals, domestic animals, birds and mankind. These powerful personnel of heaven watch the terrible effects of the curse that Satan has caused to be upon all the earth.

> *8. And the four beasts had each of them six wings about him; and they were full of eyes within; and they rest not day and night, saying, Holy, Holy, Holy, Lord God Almighty, which was, and is and is to come.*
> *9. And when those beasts give glory and honour and thanks to him that sat on the throne, who liveth for ever and ever.*
> *10. The four and twenty elders fall down before him that sat on the throne, and worship him that liveth for ever and ever, and cast their crowns before the throne, saying*
> *11. Thou art worthy, O Lord, to receive glory and honour and power: for thou hast created all things, and for thy pleasure they are and were created.*

Read Romans 8:18-22 if you think the sin curse has not affected every living thing on the earth. It has affected the ground that we walk on. It has affected mankind. It has limited our lives and caused us to be subject to disease, sickness, and death. The apostle Paul says the whole creation groaneth until now.

These four personnel of God bow down before the Lord Jesus Christ in honor and praise to Him, acknowledging that He is the only One who can relieve the burden of the curse from all living things, even the earth itself.

Sometimes we can read something once and know what it says. But it takes a lot of patience to study and understand God's Word. That, of course, is what God expects us to have, as Christians. He expects us to have time for Him and be willing to discipline ourselves. People are not conditioning themselves to receive the Word of God. Our condition of mind and submission to God has everything to do with our understanding His Word.

If someone says, "Just be still and let God talk to you" – look out! Satan is going to get on that line and start talking to you. If you want to get online with God, pick up His Word and start reading it. God communicates with us through the Holy Spirit revealed Word...through the Bible.

I believe the original manuscripts are purely the Word of God. The translations may have some flaws. The King James Version may not be more pure than any other, but there are word translations from the oldest manuscripts that can be found.

Remember – to the Philadelphian Church Age, Jesus said, *behold, I come quickly.*

If you read in Thessalonians and Corinthians you find that Jesus does not come to the earth there, but we will meet Him in the air. This is the first phase of the end time. After which, there will be seven years of tribulation on the earth.

The explanation of these seven years can be found in the book of Daniel 9:24-27:

> *24. Seventy weeks are determined upon thy people and upon thy holy city, to finish the transgression, and to make an end of sins, and to make reconciliation for iniquity, and to bring in everlasting righteousness,*

and to seal up the vision and prophecy, and to anoint the most Holy.

This is a verse of scripture that covers a lot of territory. There has not been a time in the history of man when everlasting righteousness has been brought in. So, this is not a prophecy that has been fulfilled, but it is a prophecy to be fulfilled.

25. *Know therefore and understand, that from the going forth of the commandment to restore and to build Jerusalem unto the Messiah the Prince shall be seven weeks, and threescore and two weeks: the street shall be built again, and the wall, even in troublous times.* (Look at your chart).

We know the walls were rebuilt and that it was in troubled times. The Israelite people had to keep their weapons with them as they were building the walls.

26. *And after threescore and two weeks shall Messiah be cut off, but not for himself: and the people of the prince that shall come shall destroy the city and the sanctuary; and the end thereof shall be with a flood, and unto the end of the war desolations are determined.*
27. *And he shall confirm the covenant with many for one week: and in the midst of the week he shall cause the sacrifice and the oblation to cease, and for the over- spreading of abominations he shall make it desolate, even until the consummation, and that determined shall be poured upon the desolate.*

Here we have some things that are talked about in terms of weeks. There are seventy weeks prophesied. As we look at the weeks and the chart at the end of this chapter, we find it to be extremely accurate in regards to the counting of time and the explanation of the vision Daniel received. The period of seven weeks equaled 49 (7 x 7), so seven weeks of years were 49 years. That period corresponds exactly with Biblical history. The restoration period was 49 years.

We have something else that is accurate with Biblical history. The threescore and two weeks mentioned here is 62 weeks of years, which equals 434 years. During that time there was no prophet in Israel. Those were the silent years. As we come to the end of the silent years we find John the Baptist being the last of the Old Testament prophets (Luke 16:16). Even though John the Baptist is found in the gospels of the New Testament he was the last of the Old Testament prophets. He announced the arrival of the Messiah. About three years later Jesus created the church. The church was not born...it was created. The church is not an extension of the Old Testament Patriarchal or Mosaical dispensation. It is a created vehicle of salvation for those who believe and obey the Holy Spirit breathed Word of God.

If someone says, "Do you think we are close to something happening from heaven?" I say, "Yes, I do." Do I know when? No, I do not. I think we are in the latter part of the Philadelphian Age. We have already gone into the Laodicean Age – the lukewarm age. That is why I can tell you that I think we are close. There is a strong possibility that the Lord has delayed His coming so that people can be saved.

The seven weeks (49 years) of restoring the wall and the sixty-two weeks (434 years) of silent years, equal sixty-nine weeks of the *seventy weeks determined upon thy people...* I believe you will find that the Israelite people have one more week (7 years) of pronounced judgment upon them. God will bring on some of the devastation, during this seven-year period of tribulation, and some of it will be brought on by Satan.

Once the Christians are lifted, then seven years will be focused not on Gentiles, but Jews.

I believe the scripture on the conversion of 144,000 Israelites (Revelation 7:4-8) has been misinterpreted by many people of our day. They say that we are spiritual Israel. I ask, "How can we be spiritual Israel when the Holy Spirit says there are 144,000 from the twelve tribes and He names the twelve tribes?" That means exactly what it says. The Holy Spirit has gone into too much defining for anyone to misunderstand this. We have been referred to, in the writings of the New Testament, as being spiritual Israel in a sense that it is a time of favor toward the Gentile people. The Gentiles are to carry the gospel into the world. But that time will end with the lifting of the true Christians. Jesus gave the commission to go out at the beginning of the Gentile church age and now He says, "*to him that overcometh, go out no more.*" Does that mean there will not be other Gentiles saved? No, that simply means the fullness of the Gentile age will have come. The 144,000 Jewish evangelists will go into the entire world with the gospel. They will accomplish once again what they accomplished in the first century in taking the gospel to the world. They will be, for the most part, rejected, but they will not reject Gentiles this time. They will preach to them as well as to the Jews. They will want to help everyone they possibly can. They will be lifesavers for many of the Laodicean Age. The people left here will say, "Where did I go wrong?" I would want to know, wouldn't you? Even if it takes my life...and that is what it will require because Jesus says they will sit in the throne – His throne, the martyr's throne. When the one-world leader tries to take over the world, anyone opposing him will die. Isn't that going to be a terrible decision making time? I would rather make a decision today.

I want to bring one more thing to your attention before I leave this prophecy. In your study I would like for you to read the eighth, ninth, and tenth chapters of Daniel.

We find Daniel's vision of a visitor from heaven, starting with the tenth verse of the tenth chapter.

> *10. And behold, an hand touched me, which set me upon my knees and upon the palms of my hands.*
>
> *11. And he said unto me, O Daniel, a man greatly beloved, understand the words that I speak unto thee, and stand upright: for unto thee am I now sent. And when he had spoken this word unto me, I stood trembling.*
>
> *12. Then said he unto me, Fear not, Daniel: for from the first day that thou didst set thine heart to understand, and to chasten thyself before thy God, thy words were heard, and I am come for thy words.*
>
> *13. But the prince of the kingdom of Persia withstood me one and twenty days: but, lo, Michael, one of the chief princes, came to help me; and I remained there with the kings of Persia.*

This messenger of God was not Gabriel or Michael. He was of a lesser rank. Michael, being the angel that heads the armies of God, was able to come and free him after 21 days. Apparently Satan thought this messenger had something very important to tell Daniel...so important that he stopped him for 21 days.

No doubt, all angels or heavenly messengers are more powerful than we are. So imagine what <u>we</u> are up against with Satan. We must realize his power and destructive ability.

> *14. Now I am come to make thee understand what shall befall thy people in the latter days: for yet the vision is for many days.*

It is important for us to see in this verse what the messenger told Daniel. He said this is not going to be in the near future, but many days hence.

THE SEVENTY WEEKS OF DANIEL
(Daniel 9:24-27)

Babylonian Captivity	Restoration period - 7 weeks of years - 7x7 = 49 years	No prophetic message from God 62 weeks of years 62 x 7 = 434 years	THE CHURCH AGE	Tribulation period - 1 week of years - 1 x 7 = 7 years	1000 years of peace	The King, Jesus Christ, reigning with His Kingdom united - Matt. 6
	7 weeks of years	**plus 62 weeks of yrs.**		**plus 1 week of yrs. = 70th wk.**		

Cyrus' decree to rebuild Jerusalem

Jerusalem rebuilt

Jesus Born

CHAPTER 5

1. *And I saw in the right hand of him that sat on the throne a book written within and on the backside, sealed with seven seals.*
2. *And I saw a strong angel proclaiming with a loud voice, Who is worthy to open the book, and to loose the seals thereof?*
3. *And no man in heaven, nor in earth, neither under the earth, was able to open the book, neither to look thereon.*
4. *And I wept much, because no man was found worthy to open and to read the book, neither to look thereon.*

We find in Jeremiah 32:9-12, that Jeremiah bought a piece of land. He was a prophet of God, and God had revealed to him that their land would be taken from them. God said...to assure you that the land will be restored to your people, I want you to make the deed and title to this piece of land, that is within the bounds of your tribe, to one of your heirs. He then can activate it if you leave directions for him to find it. When they did come back to the land, as God promised they would, the heir found the deed that had been placed in an earthen vessel and buried in a certain place. It was sealed and witnessed. Everything about it was legal. When the heir did activate the title then all the benefits became his.

A lot of people say, "The book mentioned in Revelation 5:1 means that Satan has the deed and title to the earth." But that is not what the Bible says. Satan has never had the deed and title to the earth and he never will. He does have possession of what God gave Adam.

I want to mention some things that Adam and Eve lost. God told them that if they ate from the forbidden tree they would surely die.

- They lost eternal life.
- God said the woman would have pain in child bearing.
- He said there would be enmity between man and every living thing.

I found out last week that we still have enmity today. I have a newborn calf. The mother was not eating with the other cows, so I went looking for her. I found the calf that had been born the night before and as I stood there looking, I saw that it appeared to be tangled in a pile of cedar brush. I thought the little thing might not be able to get out so I reached over to help it. Well, I found out there was plenty of life in it. That one day old calf jumped about a foot high, put its head down, dug in its front feet and ran at me like it was going to knock me out of its way. It did! It hit me right in the stomach. It didn't weigh but about 75 pounds so it didn't hurt me, but I thought – enmity! It's a one day old calf and I am its enemy.

- There is sorrow that will not go away. It has happened with every generation. When our loved ones depart from this earth, we that are left behind live in sorrow. Will it ever go away? It has never gone away.
- The ground does not produce well.

- God said that thorns, thistles, and pests would come with surrendering to Satan.
- He said we would labor and earn our living by the sweat of our brow.

We can see that all the miseries we face in this life come under these mentioned. The whole earth is affected by Adam's fall and we are subjected to it in this life.

Satan has access to what God allowed man to have in the beginning and lost.

As we study our Bible, we find in the Old Testament that God commanded man to make temporary sacrifices to teach him the seriousness of sin. We find that the blood of bulls and goats could not take away sin, but it was a substitute until the True sacrifice. Some people say that it was ridiculous for them to make animal sacrifices. No, it was not. It was a command from God. This was leading up to the real sacrifice, which was Jesus Christ. Without the shedding of His blood there is no remission of sins.

As we read in the fourth verse, John is having a vision from God. John is weeping over the fact that there can be no relief because no one in heaven or on earth was found worthy to open and read the book. Here is another point we want to look at. God the Father, Jesus Christ, and the Holy Spirit were not included in the searching of heaven and earth for someone to remove this curse. They are not included because God, Jesus Christ, and the Holy Spirit always were, are, and always will be. The Three possess all power, even over Satan. They are honest, straight, and just, according to God's justice system.

We know that we do not deserve forgiveness, but when God provided a way that our sins can be covered, it was in accordance with His justice system.

As we will find out later, only Jesus Christ, the Lion of the tribe of Judah, the Divine Son of God, can release these things.

It's an exciting chapter! It is allowing us to know that even John, in this vision, is weeping. He is mourning the fact that no one is able to release the affects of the curse until it is announced from heaven that the time has come for the seals to be opened. There is a promise from God that they will be opened.

> 5. *And one of the elders saith unto me, Weep not: behold, the Lion of the tribe of Juda, the Root of David, hath prevailed to open the book, and to loose the seven seals thereof.*

Who is the Lion of the tribe of Juda? JESUS CHRIST! He is the Lion of the tribe of Juda. He has prevailed to release us! If I didn't have great control I would start shouting right now! The Lion of the tribe of Juda, none other than Jesus Christ, has prevailed to open the book and to loose the seven seals that have caused and are still causing great misery, sorrow, pain, suffering and death on this earth – thank God. We have the identification here of Jesus Christ, unmistakably, in the fifth verse.

> 6. *And I beheld, and lo, in the midst of the throne and of the four beasts, and in the midst of the elders, stood a Lamb as it had been slain, having seven horns and seven eyes, which are the seven Spirits of God, sent forth into all the earth.*
> 7. *And he came and took the book out of the right hand of him that sat upon the throne.*

What a verse of scripture! ...*stood a Lamb as it had been slain*...The Bible refers to Jesus Christ as the Lamb slain for the sins of the world. What a revelation we have! ...*having seven horns*...horns of power. When we find something in the Bible about horns it is always referring to power.

What do we find concerning the number **seven**? We find that it means complete...100%. When the Holy Spirit gave the names of the seven churches He meant the complete age of the church from beginning to end. Seven means it is all there.

He has *seven horns*, which means He has all power. There is no one that has power over the Lamb that was slain. The Father, Son, and Holy Spirit are not to be compared with any created being in heaven or on earth.

...*seven eyes*...this means He does not miss one thing. As they search the earth constantly they are looking for people who will submit themselves to the Lord Jesus Christ.

When someone says, "I know what the Bible says, but I think it's this way," they are trying to take the power away from Jesus Christ. Adam and Eve wanted to take some of the power away from God. That is what Satan told them they could do. He said, "You will be like God." This is a problem we see in the world today.

We find in the seventh verse that the Lamb came and took the book from the right hand of Him that sat upon the throne. He took the book that was bound with seven seals.

We inhabitants of the earth are still bound by sin cursed conditions. These things will not go away in this life. But Jesus Christ has accomplished on the cross all that is necessary to give us the strength to face up to these things until they are removed. We are living under the binds of Satan that cause misery, pain, and death. Can anyone tell me these things have gone away? We know they have not gone away. Every time we have a funeral we know and are reminded that they have not gone away. God says He will give us the strength to bear it. We then pray to God and thank Him for the strength we have to endure these things until the Lion of the tribe of Juda, Jesus Christ, will take them away. I am not telling you that this has not been accomplished. It is just like the deed and title that was sealed in an earthen vessel for seventy years that had not been broken open and claimed. It was already done. Christ has already done all that was necessary for everyone who follows His directions to have eternal life. We are waiting to reap the benefits. With the strength that God gives me, I can bear it. I do not see how people in the world without Jesus Christ can keep going. It is no wonder to me that we have drugs rampant, sex outside of marriage and all the terrible things we see going on in the world today. They are having trouble bearing the unbearable. Let's tell them that there is Someone who will help them bear up under the pressures of this life. Those people who do not know Jesus Christ have pressure like you would not believe. Thank God that we, as Christians, have strength in Him.

> 8. *And when he had taken the book, the four beasts and four and twenty elders fell down before the Lamb, having every one of them harps, and golden vials full of odours, which are the prayers of saints.*

God has stored the prayers of the righteous as He is waiting to consummate all things. He has not ignored the prayers of the saints. A lot of prayers are not prayed according to the will of God. We find the will of God in the Bible.

> 9. *And they sung a new song, saying, Thou art worthy to take the book, and to open the seals thereof: for thou wast slain; and hast redeemed us to God by thy blood out of every kindred, and tongue, and people, and nation;*

This verse shows that the justice system of God has been satisfied.

Satan knows that his time is short. He knows that Jesus Christ has the power to take from him what he took from man. We say did God do it or did Satan do it? God allowed it, but Satan did it. God gives us the strength to endure it until our death here on earth. He will then wipe away all tears and all sorrow forever and ever.

The church is the kingdom of God and "we've no less days to sing God's praise than the hour we first begun," as long as we remain faithful to Him. So we can experience eternality here as well as there. When we get there we too will be singing a new song. We will not sing some of the songs that we sing here such as "He is Building a Castle for Me Over There," "In the Sweet By and By," or "There's Coming a Day." I don't believe that singing new songs will be a problem. Think of all the gifted songwriters that have gone on before and the ones that will be lifted from the earth. They will all be in one place – not scattered over generations of time.

10. And hast made us unto our God kings and priests: and we shall reign on the earth.

As Christians living on this earth, being in the kingdom of God, we are a kingdom of priests. We are a royal priesthood (I Peter 2:9), so we have some understanding of the responsibilities we will have in the eternal order. You might say, "It sounds like I am going to be put to work there." We will love whatever God has for us to do.

11. And I beheld, and I heard the voice of many angels round about the throne and the beasts and the elders:

When we find the word "beast" translated from the original text it always means strong ones, powerful personnel. This is hard for us to understand because Satan and his cohorts are referred to as beasts. But I find that the heav-

<u>enly</u> personnel are also referred to as beasts. In this eleventh verse, these are powerful personnel of heaven.

...and the number of them was ten thousand times ten thousand, and thousands of thousands;

God did not number these people, but He allowed us to know that it is a vast amount. It doesn't only include the saved of the earth up to that point in time, but it is all the personnel of heaven who have been anxiously awaiting the release of the sin curse that is on the earth. They are able to witness, first hand, some of the blessings.

God is able to pronounce things that are in the future as if they have already happened. If you read in the book of Isaiah about the coming of the Messiah you might say, "Had He already come?" No, but He was coming. God had already said so and He could speak of it in the present tense.

12. *Saying with a loud voice, Worthy is the Lamb that was slain to receive power, and riches, and wisdom, and strength, and honour, and glory, and blessing.*

...Worthy is the Lamb that was slain... The Old Testament tells us about the Messiah, the Lamb of God. Isaiah prophesied that He is brought as a Lamb to the slaughter. Jesus submitted himself for the crucifixion. He *was slain to receive power, riches, wisdom, strength, honor, glory, and blessing.* There will not be an end to the honor and glory of Jesus Christ.

I have a feeling that it will not take long for our gifted songwriters to come up with new songs about the blessings there. Yes, there will be wonderful singing in heaven.

13. *And every creature which is in heaven, and on the earth, and under the earth, and such as are in the sea, and all that are in them, heard I saying, Blessing, and honour, and glory, and power, be unto him that*

sitteth upon the throne, and unto the Lamb for ever and ever.

When we look at this verse of scripture, we find every living thing breathing a sigh of relief, as Jesus is about to over-power the god of this world. He is about to de-throne Satan. Every living creature in heaven will cast a vote for God and Jesus Christ. They will surrender to their authority forever and ever.

When you win an election you realize how much damage can be done by the certain percentage of people that did not vote for you. I experienced that first-hand. They never let up.

Isn't it going to be wonderful in heaven? There will not be one vote cast against God, Jesus Christ, or the Holy Spirit.

The next verse will conclude the celebration of victory for the saints.

14. And the four beasts (the four powerful beings of heaven) *said, Amen.*

As we go into the next chapter we need to remember that the four powerful beings will characterize the first four seals that are broken. Also, I want to prepare you for this...Satan is angry.

We have had some experience with wild animals that are about to be captured...they will do the unexpected. They have power that is beyond our imagination. When they see they are cornered, and there is no way to escape, they start doing all the damage they can do.

The people left here on earth will be the recipients of this hemmed up, powerful, Satanic force. The first four seals that are broken will be a picture of Satan doing what a hemmed up beast would do when it realizes there is no escape.

And the four and twenty elders fell down and worshipped him that liveth for ever and ever.

This will be the end of the celebration and I do not know how long it will last. I hope to be present. We will know more about it over there.

In the sixth chapter we will see how much Satan cares about the people who have not lived up to their commitment to Jesus Christ. He will make people think he cares about them...trying to get them to be selfish with what they have and just take care of number one. He is going to show them what it means to take care of number one – that is, himself. He does not care what happens to anyone else.

One of the hardest things for me to do in my study of this book is to keep things in chronological order. The fourth and fifth chapters are immediately after the first lifting of the living Christians, and the resurrected dead saints of both the Church Age and the Old Testament era. The offer of salvation from God is still on the earth. There is no incentive for anyone to say, "If I don't make it in the first lifting of Christians from the earth I will have another chance after that." I have told you that I think some people will be saved after the first lifting, but believe me, this will not be an incentive to stay here. How would you like to hear someone say, "You can come over here with the beast and live?" But they will not call him the beast. They are going to call him something that sounds great. He will be very deceiving. Satan's followers will say, "You can have all the comfort you want if you take the number of the beast and reject Jesus Christ." There will be many people who will do that. There is no incentive to wait – there is no second chance incentive.

Chapter 6

1. And I saw when the Lamb opened one of the seals, and I heard, as it were the noise of thunder, one of the four beasts (strong heavenly beings) *saying, Come and see.*

In other words, you are going to have a view of what Satan does on the earth. The strong heavenly being says, *Come and see.* What did they hear? They heard a noise like thunder. When the Holy Spirit records something that is loud and sounds destructive I think that is Satan letting off a roar…just like an animal before it attacks. That is to frighten as much as possible.

I remember when I took basic training in the army. We had a bayonet and there were silhouettes out there. The sergeant said, "When you go out with that bayonet you are facing a man just as you would in combat. When you strike that silhouette I want to hear you roar! I want to hear you make a noise." I remember doing that. The sergeant said, "That doesn't sound like a roar to me – you don't sound a bit dangerous! I mean I want you to sound like you are dangerous!" I always think about that when I study about Satan. He lets off a roar to let everyone know how dangerous he is and what he can do.

When the Lamb opened the first seal, Satan let off a roar.

2. And I saw, and behold a white horse: and he that sat on him had a bow; and a crown and was given unto him: and he went forth conquering, and to conquer.

Here we have some things that are going to happen immediately on the earth. Satan has to move his forces into position.

Up to 100 years ago, the horse was the most powerful thing that we had on the earth to move us into position – in battle or anywhere else. Today we probably think of planes that can carry millions of tons. This is written so that all generations of the earth should be able to understand it. So the horse is used to signify coming into power.

The white horse represents moving into power and the diplomatic procedure that will start the beginning of the tribulation period. Why does he have a bow? The bow is a weapon. But he has no ammunition. It is further indication that this leader is going to rule with diplomacy. He is given a crown, which means that he will obtain endorsement from the majority of governments on the earth.

We have the stage set for this. The governments of the world are positioning the United Nations to have power and authority over all nations. The rulers of the earth have already surrendered to them with the exception of a few. Watch the news or read the paper. You will see the Bible being fulfilled right before your eyes.

The world leader that will take over is not a good man or a person that loves people. He loves power. The best way he can get into power is to appear as a diplomat. Remember, I said he has a bow, but no arrows.

Satan will try to gain leadership through individuals that allow him to control their lives.

As we look at the world today we can easily see that there are many people allowing Satan to control them. What we must do as Christians is persuade people to let God, Jesus Christ, and the Holy Spirit, be first in their lives.

God, Jesus Christ, and the Holy Spirit are <u>as One</u>. They want us to be <u>as one</u> with Them. Jesus prayed for this in John 17.

> *3. And when he had opened the second seal, I heard the second beast say, Come and see.*

This is the heavenly view, a vision that John has from the safety of heaven, as he looks down upon the earth and is able to see what is happening.

> *4. And there went out another horse that was red: and power was given to him that sat thereon to take peace from the earth, and that they should kill one another: and there was given unto him a great sword.*

The rider on the white horse had a bow, but no arrows. The rider on this horse has a great sword. This indicates that he will use the sword to gain the position he wants.

We need to keep in mind that this period of time is the first twenty-one months of the tribulation period. The tribulation period is eighty-four months. These seven years will be the finishing of Jacob's trouble that was pronounced in the Old Testament. The prophetic clock is allowed to start at the beginning of this period.

This rider goes out and is identified as being on a red horse. The color of the horse indicates the way he will govern. The rider on the white horse says I want to look good to everyone. The rider on this horse does not have to worry about the opposition of the people. He is already in a position of power and he takes peace from the earth...*that they should kill one another.* He will have very powerful weapons of war at his disposal. He can use these on the people of the earth that will not submit to him.

We cannot forget the back-sliden condition of the Laodicean Church Age or the awakening some will have when Christians disappear from the earth. Many will repent.

Don't ever forget that God wants to save people...not destroy. He is loving, merciful, and long-suffering. He wants to save those who will condition themselves according to His Word. God could destroy the people on earth at any time and be right in doing so, but He doesn't.

In verse 4, the world leader is killing the people who will not submit to him. Satan will place this leader in a position of power over the whole world. We find out later how many they will kill.

Do you remember when Jesus said to the Laodiceans that they will share His throne? We concluded that the only throne they can possibly share with Jesus is the martyrs throne.

We have everything to gain by being in the first lifting of Christians from the earth.

This character on the red horse takes peace from the earth – he has a great sword.

5. *And when he had opened the third seal, I heard the third beast say, Come and see.* Come and view what is happening on the earth. In the safety of the arms of God, John is allowed to see what is taking place...*and I beheld, and lo a black horse; and he that sat on him had a pair of balances in his hand.*

6. *And I heard a voice in the midst of the four beasts say, A measure of wheat for a penny, and three measures of barley for a penny; and see thou hurt not the oil and the wine.*

In the fourth verse, we find war and killings. Where war has devastated a country there is always famine. The people will not be able to produce food. The war mentioned in this verse will be all over the world. This famine is going to be terrible. It will follow the killings and the opposition that the world leader has as he takes power. He will kill everyone that chooses Jesus Christ.

We see in the fifth verse that he has a pair of balances in his hand, meaning there will be a rationing of food.

We know a little bit about rationing from World War II. We had some rationing of almost all supplies, so the balances took effect then, to some extent.

These balances are going to be different and quite extensive because they will be so far reaching.

As we look at verse 6, we see that there will be people not able to make enough money in one day to buy food for one day. We read in the Bible where people could work one day and get enough food to last them for a day. That way they kind of kept even with the board, so to speak. We find scripture in the Bible that tells us of an employer paying his men at the end of a day's work. They needed the money to buy food for the day. It was one day at a time. That is a little hard for us to understand in the affluent society we live in today.

The wine and the oil are the rich people who have money and can buy. It will be impossible for those without money to get food. The rationing of food will not hurt the rich.

7. And when he had opened the fourth seal, I heard the voice of the fourth beast say, Come and see.

The fourth beast is one of the powerful heavenly beings. He says come and see how Satan is showing his dislike for the fact that he knows his time is short. Satan does not care what he does to the people of the earth. That is why it is called a tribulation period like no other.

John had a view of what will happen on the earth, as the fourth seal was opened.

8. *And I looked, and behold a pale horse: and his name that sat on him was Death, and Hell followed with him. And power was given unto them over the fourth part of the earth, to kill with sword, and with hunger, and with death, and with the beasts of the earth.*

Can you imagine this kind of person being in power of the government and in control of all things?

We find the famine, we find the scarcity of food, and we find the rich being able to make it.

Satan will give the rider power over a fourth of the earth to kill with the sword, starve the people, or terrorize in any way to gain the power he wants. He will simply kill off his opposition. We have had a little of that on the earth such as Saddam Hussein. The reports say that he even kills his own family members if they threaten his position of power. But that is in one place. Think how terrible it will be when there is someone like that sitting in control of government over the whole world.

In the first four seals that are opened Satan is throwing his last fling. He is trying to make the people of the earth as miserable as he possibly can. But who is Satan's enemy? Who does he hate? He hates God. He hates God so much that he is making war against Him. He thinks he is getting back at God.

Things take on a different look here as the last three seals are opened. It seems to me it is vengeance from God for what Satan has been doing. Notice this closely.

9. *And when he had opened the fifth seal, I saw under the altar the souls of them that were slain for the word of God, and for the testimony which they held:*

See what I'm talking about? The fifth seal does not read like the other four. This seal gives John a view of all the people who have been killed for their faith. These people who are under the altar, that have been killed, are not gone. They are simply waiting for their reward just as we who are living are waiting for our reward. These people are under the altar, the protection of God.

I would much rather preach a funeral where I feel the person was a Christian and was under the protection of God. If I know the person loved God there are many comforting words I can say. It makes me feel good to know that someone has lived in the fear of God. There are a lot of things we cannot say if they did not know God. God is *just* and we know He will give them their *just reward.*

John can see the people that are protected under the altar of God. There will be a vast number of them.

> *10. And they cried with a loud voice, saying, How long, O Lord, holy and true, dost thou not judge and avenge our blood on them that dwell on the earth?*

They cried with a loud voice. Their prayers have been: Lord, we know you are Holy and True and that vengeance is yours, but we want to know, dear Lord, how long will it be? Prayers that are not in the will of God will not be stored or answered. Prayers that are in the will of God will be answered, or stored for answering, when God's timetable is right. We cannot control God's timetable with our prayers, but He will not forget us.

They say, how long will it be?

> *11. And white robes were given unto every one of them; and it was said unto them, that they should rest yet for a little season, until their fellow-servants also and their brethren, that should be killed as they were, should be fulfilled.*

This is the Holy Spirit revelation of God's answer. He comforts them by covering them with His righteousness.

In the first twenty-one months of the tribulation period people will be going to the hills. They will have to provide food and clothing for themselves just like the old settlers had to do many years ago. They will be hard to find. They are not going to invite death. People who are faithful to God are going to be under cover.

The Holy Spirit is saying here: Wait a little season because there are more people like you who will be killed just like you were. Then God will take care of the situation.

This is the fifth seal. Satan is not the one in control here.

12. And I beheld when he had opened the sixth seal, and, lo, there was a great earthquake; and the sun became black as sackcloth of hair, and the moon became as blood.

The sixth seal brought a change in the environment. This is just one segment of the reshaping of the earth and Satan is not doing this – God is. Why is God doing this? For the same reason He does everything. He is trying to get people to repent and turn to Him. He is in the salvation of souls business, not the destruction business. The decision making time is not a lifetime. The whole period is eighty-four months. God is hastening things along to make people realize there is no security on the earth. People are putting off making a decision to accept Christ as Lord and Savior. They are not saying, "I do not believe in God or His Word." They are saying I have plenty of time; besides that, I have the security of the earth. Death can come at any time. That should hasten their decision. It doesn't matter how old a person is, they will still think they have time. I do not feel different than I did when I was ten years old, but I know my time is shorter now.

God will do everything he can to cause people to realize that time is short. Make your decision.

13. *And the stars of heaven fell unto the earth, even as a fig tree casteth her untimely figs, when she is shaken of a mighty wind.*
14. *And the heaven departed as a scroll when it is rolled together; and every mountain and island were moved out of their places.*

This earth has swamps and mountains and only one-fifth of it is usable. Mountains will be leveled and swamps filled. The earth will not look the same.

All of these things, I think, are connected with the curse that came because of Adam and Eve's sin.

15. *And the kings of the earth, and the great men, and the rich men, and the chief captains, and the mighty men, and every bondman, and every free man, hid themselves in the dens and in the rocks of the mountains;*

It is a period of time when even the dignitaries of the earth will not be able to find safety.

16. *And said to the mountains and rocks, Fall on us, and hide us from the face of him that sitteth on the throne, and from the wrath of the Lamb:*

They will say let it end. They will recognize that it is the wrath of the Lamb. God wants them to hasten their decision.

17. *For the great day of his wrath is come; and who shall be able to stand?*

CHAPTER 7

1. *And after these things I saw four angels standing on the four corners of the earth, holding the four winds of the earth, that the wind should not blow on the earth, nor on the sea, nor on any tree.*

   ...four corners of the earth,... What does John mean? We know that the earth is round, but we also know that the wind comes from four different directions. That is what the Holy Spirit is saying – four directions of the wind. We can also see, in the first verse, that things will be quiet on the earth. There will be no disruptions. Instead of limiting this to the wind I think it means there will be no great disruptions from Satan. This will be a short span of time.

2. *And I saw another angel ascending from the east, having the seal of the living God: and he cried with a loud voice to the four angels, to whom it was given to hurt the earth and the sea,*

   We find this angel as he speaks concerning the seal of the living God. A lot of people use the phrase, "I have been saved," "I have become a Christian," or "I have been sealed." We can use any of the phrases and be correct. In II Corinthians 1:21-22, the apostle Paul tells us – *God hath also*

sealed us and given the earnest of the Spirit in our hearts.
That is what takes place when someone becomes a Christian.
When a person obeys the initial steps in the plan of salvation
then that person receives the seal. It is the assurance that he,
or she, has been purchased by the blood of Christ. We can
all claim this seal as long as we remain faithful to the Lord
Jesus. We are guaranteed by the Word of God that He has
purchased us by the blood of Jesus. The people, during the
tribulation period, that choose the Lord Jesus Christ will also
be sealed.

> 3. *Saying, Hurt not the earth, neither the sea, nor the*
> *trees, till we have sealed the servants of our God in*
> *their foreheads.*

Having the seal in their foreheads will be a testimony to
the rest of the world that they are Christians.

The people of the world are those who reject Jesus Christ.
They are playing havoc in the world today and will be a more
destructive force during the tribulation period than ever
before.

We have never been persecuted for our faith here in
America. It will be a strange thing when people are singled out
and persecuted because of their acceptance of Jesus Christ.

Everything is quiet on the earth until the sealing of
the servants of God. All of this takes place during the
first quarter of the tribulation period – the first twenty-one
months.

We have been able to see things happen on the earth such
as the Iron Curtain that separated Germany from communist Russia. I never would have thought we were so close to
seeing the wall come down, but things can develop quickly.

4. And I heard the number of them which were sealed: and there were sealed an hundred and forty and four thousand of all the tribes of the children of Israel.

This verse tells us that the sealing will be primarily Jews that are scattered throughout the world.

I would like to know the Old Testament scripture as well as Ben Alexander knows it. When he became a Christian he had no trouble with the New Testament because he had such knowledge of the schoolmaster.

These 144,000 will have a good understanding of the Old Testament scripture, so there will be a great influx of Jews accepting the Lord Jesus Christ as Savior. Once they do, the New Testament will be easy for them because they have been taught the Old Testament scripture. In order to understand the New Testament properly we have to know the Old Testament. The Jews already know the Old Testament. These people will not be the Israel that we read about in the paper that became a nation in 1948.

I read in the paper last week that eight hundred thousand Jews are in inter-faith marriages in America. One couple that was interviewed said they decided to raise their children in one faith. Their decision was that the husband would convert to the Christian faith. When I say Christian faith I am not saying Christian church. If eight hundred thousand inter-faith marriages of Jew and Gentile have taken place in America, I would like to see the statistics from other countries. According to the Rabbi, that was taking part in the inter-faith marriages, this has not happened before on such a large scale.

The true Christians who believed there is *one Lord, one faith, one baptism, one God and Father of all, who is above all, and through all, and in you all* (Ephesians 4:5,6), will have already been called from the earth.

5. *Of the tribe of Juda were sealed twelve thousand. Of the tribe of Reuben were sealed twelve thousand. Of the tribe of Gad were sealed twelve thousand.*
6. *Of the tribe of Asher were sealed twelve thousand. Of the tribe of Nep-tha-lim were sealed twelve thousand. Of the tribe of Ma-nas-ses were sealed twelve thousand.*
7. *Of the tribe of Simeon were sealed twelve thousand. Of the tribe of Levi were sealed twelve thousand. Of the tribe of Is-sa-char were sealed twelve thousand.*
8. *Of the tribe of Za-bu-lon were sealed twelve thousand. Of the tribe of Joseph were sealed twelve thousand. Of the tribe of Benjamin were sealed twelve thousand.*

The twelve tribes are named. I find that these twelve names do not coincide with the twelve tribes mentioned in the Old Testament – not 100%. As I came to the name Dan, I found that his name is not included in this listing. Read Judges, the entire eighteenth chapter, and you will find that Dan became an adulterous tribe. This is the only reason I could find that Manasseh replaces him. But notice, the Bible says there will be twelve thousand from each of the twelve tribes. Some people say we are spiritual Israel since we are the church of the Lord Jesus Christ. I will agree that there is some reference in the New Testament to us as spiritual Israel. Who is Israel? They are a people favored of God in the sense that they have acknowledged and loved Him. Taking this into account I can understand that He has referred to us as spiritual Israel. But if I apply this to the Christians (where He speaks of spiritual Israel) I begin to think, "Would the Holy Spirit go into such detail to name the twelve tribes and if I am spiritual Israel what tribe am I from?" I am not an Israelite.

Since the Laodicean Church Age will be left, they will have to do some soul-searching. Many will convert to one

Lord, one faith, and one baptism. It is not going to be a good time. The people who are converted to the Lord Jesus Christ will do so at their detriment as far as the government of the world is concerned. Many will be put to death. Do you remember the prayers? They say, "God, how long are you going to allow this to go on?" He said, "Wait a little while because there are still people on the earth who will die just like you did." See how that ties in?

People are funny. They say, "That would be a second chance; that wouldn't be fair." Whatever God does is fair. You know what He did about the people who worked all day or one hour – He said it is mine to give.

Just to show you how people are...when I worked at GE, the company announced a window for early retirement. Anyone 55 years of age with 25 years of service could retire with no reduction in pension. A maintenance man said, "Is there going to be another window? If there is, I'm not going to take this one." The company said, "As far as our plans are now, there will not be another one." The guy did not want to miss it, but he didn't want to take it if they were going to have another one within a year. He decided that he could not turn it down. About a year later the company offered another window. The maintenance man came in and said he was going to file a lawsuit. He said, "This is not fair! They told me they had no other plans for a retirement window. If they hadn't told me that, I would not have taken it. I would have kept on working and made more money." See how people think? This is the way they think about God so many times. This is the way they are thinking when they say this will be a second chance for those who are in the second phase of the first resurrection. This will be something God should not offer the people, they say.

We have to keep in mind that the false prophet will begin to deceive the world. Who is the false prophet? Is he going to put a sign across his chest that says "false prophet?" No!

True believers will be able to detect that he is a counterfeit. He will say, "I am the true leader." The sad thing about it is, he will say, "I am the world religious leader. I have the truth and I will tell you what to do now. Would I tell you wrong? I am your religious leader." No doubt, he will deny the lifting of the Christians and say that the disappearance is because of something else. Hopefully we will not be here. The false religious leader (false prophet) will deceive those who do not know and have not searched the Word of God. We, as Christians, are a royal priesthood and a royal priesthood has a responsibility to God. We cannot say, "I think I will be all right as long as I follow my leader." We cannot think like that. We are to think, "I must know what God's Word says." This will prepare us for any situation.

9. After this I beheld, and lo, a great multitude, which no man could number, of all nations, and kindreds, and people, and tongues, stood before the throne, and before the Lamb, clothed with white robes, and palms in their hands;

I want to identify this great number of all nations, and kindreds, and people, and tongues that stood before the throne and before the Lamb, clothed with white robes and palms in their hands. These are the people I told you about who are of the Laodicean Age. They will remember the sayings of the faithful people of God who have already been called off the earth. These are the people from all kindreds, tongues, and nations who have died for their faith including the 144,000 and other Jewish converts. God will not select them at random or against their will. He will not supersede their will in order to save them. They will be sealed when they accept the Lord Jesus Christ and remain faithful to Him.

I have heard some people say there will be a great revival on the earth and that we are right on the verge of it. I agree that there will be a great revival. It will not be initiated by Gentiles, but by Jewish converts.

We have this vast group of people lifted in the second phase of the first resurrection and they are standing before the throne of God.

Many people think chapter 7:10-12 is a repeat of the fourth chapter, verses 9-11. It is not. I will show you that this is a different group of people. In Chapter 4:9-11, we find:

And when those beasts give glory and honor and thanks to him that sat on the throne, who liveth for ever and ever,

The four and twenty elders fall down before him that sat on the throne, and worship him that liveth for ever and ever, and cast their crowns before the throne, saying,

Thou art worthy, O Lord, to receive glory and honour and power: for thou hast created all things, and for thy pleasure they are and were created.

Then we come back to this group of people in chapter 7:10-12:

10. *And cried with a loud voice, saying, Salvation to our God which sitteth upon the throne, and unto the Lamb.*
11. *And all the angels stood round about the throne, and about the elders and the four beasts, and fell before the throne on their faces, and worshipped God,*
12. *Saying, Amen: Blessing, and glory, and wisdom, and thanksgiving, and honour, and power, and might, be unto our God for ever and ever. Amen.*

We have the same setting, we have the same place, the same heavenly beings, but we have a different time – the second phase of the first resurrection.

Verse 13 points out the difference. It is not the same group.

> *13. And one of the elders answered, saying unto me, What are these which are arrayed in white robes? And whence came they?*

I want to mention here that the apostle John was a Jew and he lived under the Old Testament Mosaical dispensation. He studied the prophets all his life. He knew who those people were. He also lived during what we call the fullness of the Gentiles, so he knew who those people were as well. But John does not know who these people are. The elder asks John who these people are so that John would know and we would know. It points out the fact that this is a different group – a different time.

> *14. And I said unto him, Sir, thou knowest. And he said to me, These are they which came out of great tribulation, and have washed their robes, and made them white in the blood of the Lamb.*

A great tribulation is talked about here. The tribulation has already started. A quarter of the tribulation has already passed. These are the people that will be in the second lifting of the first resurrection. John gets them identified, for him and for us.

> *15. Therefore are they before the throne of God, and serve him day and night in his temple: and he that sitteth on the throne shall dwell among them.*
> *16. They shall hunger no more, neither thirst any more; neither shall the sun light on them, nor any heat.*
> *17. For the Lamb which is in the midst of the throne shall feed them, and shall lead them unto living fountains*

of waters: and God shall wipe away all tears from their eyes.

We, who take part in the first lifting and those who take part in the second lifting of the first resurrection, will have all the blessings of heaven. The sorrow that does not go away, here on earth, will not be in heaven. It will never be again.

CHAPTER 8

1. And when he had opened the seventh seal, there was silence in heaven about the space of half an hour.

The Holy Spirit is letting us know that at this time there will be a brief silence in heaven.

2. And I saw the seven angels which stood before God; and to them were given seven trumpets.

They were given seven trumpets. This is what is called the trumpet judgment. Just think...at this point on the earth there is not a soul who has acknowledged the Lord Jesus Christ...not a soul. All the rest are gone. Wouldn't you hate to live on the earth under the influence of total wickedness? The false prophet will still be here. There will be a one world political leader. The one world leader will recognize there are still some religious people on the earth. I did not say Christians, I said religious people. These religious people will be putting all their trust in the false prophet. He will not love the people, but the attention and authority. He will draw people away from the world leader. Human beings are spiritual by nature. It will be a sad situation because these people will not be following the Truth, the Word of God. They will depend completely on a religious leader. There will be a large number of them, so the world political leader will not be able to get the control he wants. He will say, "That prophet! He is the one standing in my way. I cannot get rid of Him because so many have faith in Him. I know what I'll do – I'll incorporate Him into my government." This is speculation right now, but I will show you later where it is fact. The world leader will say, "If I show my approval of this prophet, the people will be more supportive of my government." This will draw the people to these two men. Later there will be three. When I get to that point I will talk about the numbers 6-6-6.

> *3. And another angel came and stood at the altar, having a golden censer; and there was given unto him much incense, that he should offer it with the prayers of all saints upon the golden altar which was before the throne.*

You remember, I said the people that pray under the altar will have been put to death for their faith in the Lord Jesus Christ? They will say, "God, how long will you hold off your vengeance?" He says, "Wait a little while longer." These prayers have been stored. Here is where prayers are brought back. God is not going to ignore His saints who have died in such a miserable way.

At one time I asked myself, "How will there ever be a one-world religion?" Now it is pretty evident. When people have a certain belief they don't seem to want to change. No one will <u>have</u> to change; they will continue to believe what they <u>want</u> to believe. The stage is being set for the one-world religion. You hear it every where you go: "Do not say a word about another person's belief; one is as good as the other." It is important that we clean up our belief with the Word of God, that we get rid of a belief that is contrary to His Word. Sometimes people are too proud to admit their belief is not according to the Holy Spirit revealed Word in the Bible. As we study and rightly divide the Word of Truth (the Bible) and see that we have been wrong in our belief, we must be willing to change, according to the Divine measure.

4. *And the smoke of the incense, which came with the prayers of the saints, ascended up before God out of the angel's hand.* (The prayers of the saints are being answered now.)
5. *And the angel took the censer, and filled it with fire of the altar, and cast it into the earth: and there were voices, and thunderings, and lightnings, and an earthquake.*

The angel filled the censer with fire from the altar. The decision for this to happen will be made in heaven, but it is going to take place on earth. The censer filled with fire was cast to the earth *and there were voices, and thunderings, and lightnings, and an earthquake.* Thunderings are always associated with judgment. The people on earth who have rejected God are about to be judged. They are going to suffer. God will take vengeance. Even though the offer of salvation from God will still be available, the people who are left here will make the decision to either follow the world political leader and/or false prophet or they will make no decision at all.

As we get a little farther into our study I think we will find that the people who choose the world leader or the false prophet will be marked.

We say that making no decision at all is saying "no" to God, but in reality we know that does not carry through 100%. People wait many years sometimes before making a decision.

The people who have not made a decision will be pressured by the world leader and the false prophet to reject the Word of God.

6. And the seven angels which had the seven trumpets prepared themselves to sound.

The blowing of the trumpets will mark the time when disaster starts to happen on the earth. God will still be concerned for the people who have not made a decision.

7. The first angel sounded, and there followed hail and fire mingled with blood, and they were cast upon the earth: and the third part of the trees was burnt up, and all green grass was burnt up.

This is what happens on the earth when the first angel sounds the trumpet. Fire mingled with blood will be cast upon the earth and the third part of the trees and all the green grass will be *burnt up*. Trees are very important to us here on earth. They take in poisonous carbon monoxide and change it to oxygen that we can breathe. Trees and vegetation clean our air. When a third part of the trees and all the green grass is *burnt up* just think what an effect it will have on the people of the earth.

8. And the second angel sounded, and as it were a great mountain burning with fire was cast into the sea: and the third part of the sea became blood:

As the second angel sounds the trumpet, we see that a third of the sea will be polluted. We do not realize, I'm afraid, how much we depend on vegetation and the seas as we live here. God wants us to understand that we cannot sustain ourselves. The Almighty God sustains us.

Many people are placing their trust in the things of this world and in themselves. Satan doesn't want them to think of how insecure they are without God, so he tries to keep them busy. It's not wrong for us to enjoy the good things while we are here, but God does not want us to let those things turn our attention away from Him. He wants us to realize that our security is not on this earth.

> *9. And the third part of the creatures which were in the sea, and had life, died; and the third part of the ships were destroyed.*

Nothing can live in the polluted water, so a third of the sea creatures will die. Ships located in the area of the sea that is turned to blood will be destroyed.

> *10. And the third angel sounded, and there fell a great star from heaven, burning as it were a lamp, and it fell upon the third part of the rivers, and upon the fountains of waters;*

As the third angel sounds, we see that a third part of the rivers and the fountains of waters will be polluted.

Many people depend on underground water. I was talking to someone a few days ago who has a big outfit for digging water wells. Various cities call him and say, "We want you to dig a well for us so we can supply our whole city with water." A lot of the cities depend on rivers for their water, but others depend on an underground water supply. Many of us in rural areas have depended on an underground water supply for years and years. It is hard for us to actually fathom the ground beneath us having all those veins of pure running water, 100 to 200 feet down. In some parts of the United States they have to go 300 to 400 feet down to find plenty of water.

> *11. And the name of the star is called Wormwood: and the third part of the waters became wormwood; and*

many men died of the waters, because they were made bitter.

In other words, a third part of the waters will be undrinkable. Man will have no control over these things.

12. *And the fourth angel sounded, and the third part of the sun was smitten, and the third part of the moon, and the third part of the stars; so as the third part of them was darkened, and the day shone not for a third part of it, and the night likewise.*

The interruption of the lights of the heavens will effect a third part of the day and a third part of the night.

13. *And I beheld, and heard an angel flying through the midst of heaven, saying with a loud voice, Woe, woe, woe, to the inhabiters of the earth by reason of the other voices of the trumpet of the three angels, which are yet to sound.*

Something we have to keep in mind is that in the book of Revelation evil messengers of Satan are called angels and heavenly, righteous messengers of God are called angels. These are God's angels, doing His bidding. In the thirteenth verse we see the angel having pity on the inhabitants of the earth. We cannot imagine the misery that will come upon *the inhabiters of the earth.*

If there has ever been an evangelistic book, I think it is the book of Revelation. It is evangelistic in the sense that it shows the love of God, but it shows that He is not going to wink at evil. He is a loving God, but He is not going to tolerate His Word being ignored. There is plenty of evidence throughout the Bible that tells us this.

God wants us to be thankful to Him for all the good things we have on this earth.

Ephesians, Chapter 6:12-17: *For we wrestle not against flesh and blood, but against principalities, against powers, against the rulers of the darkness of this world, against spiritual wickedness in high places. Wherefore take unto you the whole armour of God, that ye may be able to withstand in the evil day, and having done all, to stand. Stand therefore, having your loins girt about with truth, and having on the breastplate of righteousness; And your feet shod with the preparation of the gospel of peace; Above all, taking the shield of faith, wherewith ye shall be able to quench all the fiery darts of the wicked. And take the helmet of salvation, and the sword of the Spirit, which is the Word of God.*

No one can say that the Holy Spirit has not warned us about our enemy. Evil influences are in the world as we see clearly defined here. But we have an antidote: we have a shield, which is our faith in Jesus Christ. He and our knowledge of Him is our shield of faith. People that are without Jesus Christ do not know what they are subject to in this evil world. We can help them to have the shield. Satan can over power us. He can and will enter our minds and hearts if we let our shield of faith down, if we do not continue to study and know the Word of God, which is our sword of the Spirit.

Matthew, Chapter 12:43-45: *When the unclean spirit is gone out of a man, he walketh through dry places, seeking rest, and findeth none. Then he saith, I will return into my house from whence I came out; and when he is come, he findeth it empty, swept and garnished. Then goeth he, and taketh with himself seven other spirits more wicked than himself, and they enter in and dwell there: and the last state*

*of that man is worse than the first. Even so shall it be also
unto this wicked generation.*

There are many people today who say that evil spirits no
longer exist. I always say, "Show me in the Bible where this
ended – that they no longer exist." The evil spirits cannot
penetrate our shield of faith in Jesus Christ. There is more
than one evil spirit; there are multiples that can take over
the life and thought pattern of an individual. I think that is
why we see so much wickedness in the world. These people
may not have reached the point where they cannot accept the
Lord Jesus Christ. The evil thought patterns and lifestyles
can be put behind them. They can do that – and until they do,
the evilness will continue with them.

II Peter, Chapter 2:4: *For if God spared not the angels
that sinned, but cast them down to hell, and delivered them
into chains of darkness, to be reserved unto judgment;*

I don't think you can beat the King James Version on the
translation of this verse of scripture. The New International
interprets this verse for us and I don't think they should do
that. The NIV says, "...to be reserved until **their** judgment."
"Their" is not the right word, according to the oldest manuscripts. The King James Version is right in saying "*unto*,"
meaning "**until**" judgment. It cannot be "their" judgment
because they are already judged.

We have to look at these scriptures and realize they are
there for us to study and understand. We cannot ignore the
Bible and expect God to forgive us when we say, "I just
didn't know." When we find out it is there, we have to deal
with it. We have to deal with God's Word – this is why He
gave it to us.

The last scripture for the foundation of what I am going to say is found in Jude, Chapter 1:6. *And the angels which kept not their first estate, but left their own habitation, he hath reserved in everlasting chains under darkness unto the judgment of the great day.*

This is a very, very important scripture. I think, even though Jude wrote only one chapter in his book, he has packed it with power. Of course, the Holy Spirit revealed this to him.

Please note how closely associated all these verses of scripture are in the New Testament. Remember these scriptures as we continue with Revelation.

CHAPTER 9

1. *And the fifth angel sounded, and I saw a star fall from heaven unto the earth: and to him was given the key of the bottomless pit.*
2. *And he opened the bottomless pit; and there arose a smoke out of the pit, as the smoke of a great furnace; and the sun and the air were darkened by reason of the smoke of the pit.*
3. *And there came out of the smoke locusts upon the earth: and unto them was given power, as the scorpions of the earth have power.*
4. *And it was commanded them that they should not hurt the grass of the earth, neither any green thing, neither any tree; but only those men which have not the seal of God in their foreheads.*

We read here of the bottomless pit and the angel who is obviously a powerful force. This angel will have charge of the bottomless pit. I will tell you, based on scriptures we have just read, who is in the bottomless pit.

I think there will be degrees of reward for the saved. We read that there will be greater condemnation for some people, so this tells us there will be different degrees of punishment.

We have read about the evil spirits that are loose on the earth without body. I think we are all familiar with the man of Gadarene that was possessed with many demons. They were tormenting him. The evil spirits, addressing Jesus through the voice of the man said, *"What have I to do with thee, Jesus, thou Son of God most high? I beseech thee, torment me not"* (Luke 8:28). The unclean spirits besought Him that He would suffer them to go into the herd of swine. You remember the story.

The scorpions coming out of the pit (being evil spirits) do not have human bodies. They are scorpions just like the Bible says. They are spirits of the evil angels that kept not their first estate (Jude, verse 6). They were kept in chains of darkness until "the" judgment, not "their" judgment. <u>Their</u> judgment is already over.

Aren't you glad that we can take part in the first lifting? I do not want to be here. We do not <u>have</u> to be here. Even some people who are not Christians say, "How much more evil can the world become?" Let's tell them, "It can get a lot worse."

I cringe at the thought of allowing people to be in my presence, leave my presence, and still not know the Lord Jesus Christ...still not know that He has prepared a way of escape.

God put these evil beings away, so they would not have access to the world, for our benefit.

The fourth verse says, *...it was commanded them that they should not hurt the grass of the earth, neither any green thing, neither any tree; but only those men which have not the seal of God in their foreheads.*

I said that after the second lifting there is no one left on the earth that has made a decision for the Lord. The angel said, *...those who do not have the seal of God.* We know what the seal of God is. We have already talked abut that. It is someone that has made a decision for God. After all those bad things happen on the earth there will be people that choose God instead of Satan. They will be spared the terrible things that take place. We can be thankful for that.

Those who have not made a decision for the Lord Jesus Christ, at that point in time, will suffer the consequence of the locusts that are released from the bottomless pit.

I wanted to show the scriptural backing for what I have said and I believe I have furnished it. It would not have made much sense if I had said these things without scripture to back it up.

Some people say that evil spirits cannot be in anything but humans. The scripture shows us, when Jesus allowed the demons to go into the swine, that they can possess the body of animals as well.

> 5. *And to them it was given that they should not kill them, but that they should be tormented five months: and their torment was as the torment of a scorpion, when he striketh a man.*
> 6. *And in those days shall men seek death, and shall not find it; and shall desire to die, and death shall flee from them.*

The people will be in such torment that they will want to die, but cannot. Evil and torment will be everywhere. There will be no escape. We say, many times, when a Christian has been ravaged with disease and pain that they were released in death – it was a blessing for them to go on. It is a blessing that allows us to be released from a body that is corruptible.

> 7. *And the shapes of the locusts were like unto horses prepared unto battle; and on their heads were as it were crowns like gold, and their faces were as the faces of men.*

8. *And they had hair as the hair of women, and their teeth were as the teeth of lions.*
9. *And they had breastplates, as it were breastplates of iron; and the sound of their wings was as the sound of chariots of many horses running to battle.*
10. *And they had tails like unto scorpions, and there were stings in their tails: and their power was to hurt men five months.*

This is a description of the way they will look – the way they will torment mankind. It will last five months.

11. *And they had a king over them, which is the angel of the bottomless pit, whose name in the Hebrew tongue is Abaddon, but in the Greek tongue hath his name Apollyon.*

As we look at this verse of scripture, we find a king over them. I think this will be Satan. We have here the Hebrew and Greek word for it, which means the same thing – the Prince of Darkness.

12. *One woe is past; and, behold, there come two woes more hereafter.*

The false prophet will do miracles that will astonish everyone. God proved His power, His Son, and His Word by miracles. Satan is going to counterfeit what God did. The false prophet will say, "I'm the prophet of God." He is going to deceive people when he says this. The Holy Spirit identifies him to Christians as a false prophet, but he will be able to deceive people who do not know or have the Word of God. He will do this with miracles, signs and wonders. Will they be fake miracles? No! The Bible says that he will do miracles...and they will not be false miracles. He will have that to add more power to his influence in the world. The false prophet will not have anything to do with the fact that this woe is passed. I think (speculating) that he will say, "See what I've done – I've stopped the scorpions. Look what else I can do. Look how powerful I am in the world. You should bow down to me." I think he will claim anything that will draw people to him.

13. *And the sixth angel sounded, and I heard a voice from the four horns of the golden altar which is before God,*

14. *Saying to the sixth angel which had the trumpet, Loose the four angels which are bound in the great river Euphrates.*

15. *And the four angels were loosed, which were prepared for an hour, and a day, and a month, and a year, for to slay the third part of men.*

16. *And the number of the army of the horsemen were two hundred thousand thousand: and I heard the number of them.*

17. *And thus I saw the horses in the vision, and them that sat on them, having breastplates of fire, and of jacinth, and brimstone: and the heads of the horses were as the heads of lions; and out of their mouths issued fire and smoke and brimstone.*

18. *By these three was the third part of men killed, by the fire, and by the smoke, and by the brimstone, which issued out of their mouths.*

19. *For their power is in their mouth, and in their tails: for their tails were like unto serpents, and had heads, and with them they do hurt.*

20. *And the rest of the men which were not killed by these plagues yet repented not of the works of their hands, that they should not worship devils, and idols of gold,*

*and silver, and brass, and stone, and of wood: which
neither can see, nor hear, nor walk:*

*21. Neither repented they of their murders, nor of their
sorceries, nor of their fornication, nor of their thefts.*

In this chapter we see that the scorpions are released first.
As the sixth angel sounds, there will be evil spirits released
out of the river Euphrates. They have been kept there
because of their destructive nature. They will be loosed and
prepared for the hour, day, month and year. If this does not
convince people that they cannot be self-sufficient, then the
second loosening of evil spirits on the world should. But the
scripture says that even after this, no one repented, no one
acknowledged God, and they continued to worship devils,
idols of gold, silver, brass, stone and wood.

We have a little taste of that in the world today. Some
people say: "I don't have time to study the Bible; I can't
understand it; I don't have time for worship; I am so busy;
I have spent so much on recreational equipment." There is
nothing wrong with working or enjoying things, but there
is something wrong with allowing anything to come before
God...the worship of our God.

If people will study the book of Revelation, as well as
the rest of the Bible, this will surely cause them to realize
that they must be prepared to meet Jesus...either in death or
when He comes back.

We need to reach people. We live in the most glorious
time that has ever been. We have the opportunity to escape
all these terrible things that are going to happen. Heaven
will be great, but to find out we don't have to face any of
these awful things that will happen on the earth is a double
blessing.

CHAPTER 10

1. *And I saw another mighty angel come down from heaven, clothed with a cloud: and a rainbow was upon his head, and his face was as it were the sun, and his feet as pillars of fire:*
2. *And he had in his hand a little book open: and he set his right foot upon the sea, and his left foot on the earth,*

This angel is a powerful administrator of God who is given power over land and sea. The little book is the subject of his mission. All living things, in the sea and on the earth, will be affected.

3. *And cried with a loud voice, as when a lion roareth: and when he had cried, seven thunders uttered their voices.*

His voice will be heard around the world. Every person will know of his appearance. The *seven thunders uttered their voices.* Seven thunders...the complete judgment of God.

4. *And when the seven thunders had uttered their voices, I was about to write: and I heard a voice from heaven saying unto me, Seal up those things which the seven thunders uttered, and write them not.*

This is one thing that God has sealed up from us. There is no need to guess what happens here because it is sealed from us. The only way anyone can know, I suppose, is to be here when this affects the earth. I hope and pray that we will not be here during this awful time. It must be something that is very frightening because the Holy Spirit said, *seal up those things...and write them not.*

5. *And the angel which I saw stand upon the sea and upon the earth lifted up his hand to heaven,*
6. *And sware by him that liveth for ever and ever, who created heaven, and the things that therein are, and the earth, and the things that therein are, and the sea, and the things which are therein, that there should be time no longer:*

I think the King James Version has a bad translation here. The New International Version has a better translation – there should be "no more delay." The oldest manuscripts say, "No more delay." The King James translation, "time no more," cannot fit because there is time after this. Jesus Christ, the Son of God, came to this earth, suffered, bled and died. He satisfied God's justice and judgment, as far as sin is concerned, for those who will accept and obey Him. From that time to this, God has had time on delay. But it will not be on delay, at this point in time, as we study in the book of Revelation and see that God is bringing things to a close. He is telling us things that will happen before the end. God will not allow this world to stand forever in sin – He will not do that. We have been blessed with the mercy of God. Every person in the world can be blessed with the mercy of God if they will accept His Son as Lord and Savior...accept Him as the Divine Son of God and make Him the Lord of their life. There will be *no more delay.*

> 7. *But in the days of the voice of the seventh angel, when he shall begin to sound, the mystery of God should be finished, as he hath declared to his servants the prophets.*

As we read the last half of the twelfth chapter of Daniel, we see where Daniel prophesied that these things would happen in the end time…a long way off.

When the Holy Spirit says these things were declared to the prophets He is not talking about the apostles. We know the apostles were prophets of God as well as others in the New Testament who had been empowered with special gifts. Here, the Holy Spirit is referring to the prophets of the Old Testament.

> 8. *And the voice which I heard from heaven spake unto me again, and said, Go and take the little book which is open in the hand of the angel which standeth upon the sea and upon the earth.* (John is to go to the angel and take the little book, which is open.)
> 9. *And I went unto the angel, and said unto him, Give me the little book. And he said unto me, Take it, and eat it up; and it shall make thy belly bitter, but it shall be in thy mouth sweet as honey.*

This is a little difficult for us to understand, but it was a way of communication from God to man in Old Testament times. God would reveal something to the prophets and on more than one occasion He told them to eat it. We refer to the Word of God, even today, as the Bread of Life. We say, "We have come together today to receive the Bread of Life." We can eat and digest it or we can refuse it – whichever we want to do. If we eat it, so to speak, that means we have understood it; we have taken it into our lives. Once we have taken it into our lives we find that this places a responsibility upon us to go out and put it forth to someone else. That is what God told the prophets to do. He spoke to them, told them to "eat it" and to then go out and tell the people.

The receiving of God's Word is very sweet. We find, in the ninth verse of Chapter 10, that the receiving of God's Word is the sweet part.

Many times, when we tell people what God says in His Word, they do not want to hear it. That is the bitter part. We have a problem in the religious world telling people something they do not want to hear. I would much rather tell someone what they want to hear, but sometimes I know that what they do not want to hear is what they need. I cannot allow the bitterness of it to keep me from telling them. Jesus is my Lord. God has provided mercy for me, so how can I not tell them? That is what he is talking about here...*take it, and eat it*. In other words, educate yourselves with it.

When we teach someone the Word of God we cannot say, "You have to understand it and accept it; you have to digest it and make it a part of your life." They do not have to! Everyone has a freedom of will. We must do what God says, even if it is sometimes unpleasant.

All things will be wonderful when we reach the eternal shores, but until we do, everything may not be exactly the way we want it. We may not like to get out of bed and make ourselves ready to assemble for worship, but we do it because we know that God has told us in His Word to not forsake the assembly. If we love Him we will keep His commandments.

> 10. *And I took the little book out of the angel's hand, and ate it up; and it was in my mouth sweet as honey: and as soon as I had eaten it, my belly was bitter.*

Teaching the Truth is not the sweetest thing for me to do, especially when I know that people do not want to hear it.

John is verifying what the Holy Spirit told him. I believe the little book John received from the angel was a book of prophecy and I think it was bitter for him to put forth. It was both bitter and sweet...just as the proclaiming of the pure message of God is both bitter and sweet for every human being on earth.

11. *And he said unto me, Thou must prophesy again before many peoples, and nations, and tongues, and kings.*

John is prophesying to everyone that studies this Revelation of Jesus Christ, which is a part of the New Testament. It has been available for every tongue, every nation of people, and for kings. We are to take that message to the world. The Holy Spirit prophesied to John and John recorded it, undiluted. For 2,000 years John has been prophesying before many peoples, nations, tongues and kings.

CHAPTER 11

1. And there was given me a reed like unto a rod: and the angel stood, saying, Rise, and measure the temple of God, and the altar, and them that worship therein,

This primarily concerns the last seven years – the fulfillment of Daniel's prophecy; the nation of Israel's trouble that would be for seventy years. The seventy years has not been completely fulfilled. This is talking about the final seven years of Israel's trouble. John receives a rod to measure the temple.

According to newspaper reports the Jews are receiving funds to rebuild the temple. I am not telling you that it will be according to the will of God that they build another temple because this is rejecting Christ. I think the Jews will rebuild the temple and I believe the first verse of chapter 11 refers to this. But they do not possess the land on which they want to build the temple. The Arabs have possession of it at this time and the structure they have built there is called the Dome of the Rock. It is where Abraham was willing to offer Isaac as a sacrifice…Mount Moriah. This spot of ground means something to the Jews and they will not stop until they get it.

John was told to measure the temple of God. When we talk about spiritual measurements, what do we do? We measure our belief by the Divine measuring rod. When we want to find out if we are right, spiritually, we go to the Bible. The angel said measure the temple, measure the altar, and measure them that worship therein. God is saying...they do not measure up.

The people are anti-God when they say they love God, but reject Jesus Christ. It's like I said earlier, the Restoration Movement has turned into a Christ-centered movement. No one wants to say Restoration Movement any more...they want to say, Christ-centered. If their belief is not Bible based, it is not Christ-centered.

The Jews may build a temple as magnificent as the one they had in Solomon's day, but still it will not measure up. The people that worship in it will not measure up.

I like the King James translation on this – *And them that worship therein.* I think this is about as close as you can get to the original translation.

2. *But the court which is without the temple leave out, and measure it not; for it is given unto the Gentiles: and the holy city shall they tread under foot forty and two months.*

The world is made up of Jew and Gentile. It was that way in the Old Testament, it has been that way through the New Testament, and it is still that way today. Actually, we have only two nationalities of people, although we divide them into many different nationalities. Anyone who is not a Jew is a Gentile.

Our faithfulness to God will deliver us from the tribulation period.

At the beginning of the first three and one-half years a peace treaty will be signed. This will allow the Jews to choose the borders of the Holy Land and will allow them to once again take possession of the place called Mount Moriah. Three and one-half years into the tribulation period the Gentile world will break the treaty. That is when they will tread the Holy City under foot...for *forty and two months,* which is three and one-half years.

> 3. *And I will give power unto my two witnesses, and they shall prophesy a thousand two hundred and threescore days, clothed in sackcloth.*
> 4. *These are the two olive trees, and the two candlesticks standing before the God of the earth.*

Zechariah, Chapter 4:11-14 is prophesying what will come to pass: *Then answered I, and said unto him, What are these two olive trees upon the right side of the candlestick and upon the left side thereof? And I answered again, and said unto him, What be these two olive branches which through the two golden pipes empty the golden oil out of themselves? And he answered me and said, Knowest thou not what these be? And I said, No, my lord. Then said he, These are the two anointed ones, that stand by the Lord of the whole earth.*

These...two anointed ones; I think this is in reference to the two witnesses, or the two candlesticks, or the two olive trees.

In Romans 11:24-27, Paul is speaking, through the Divine guidance of the Holy Spirit, in regard to Israel. This is a chapter that hardly anyone uses as a text for teaching. I think it is misunderstood by many: *For if thou wert cut out of the olive tree which is wild by nature, and wert grafted contrary to nature into a good olive tree: how much more shall these, which be the natural branches, be grafted into their own olive tree? For I would not, brethren, that ye should be ignorant of this mystery, lest ye should be wise in your own conceits; that blindness in part is happened to Israel, until the fullness of the Gentiles be come in. And so all Israel shall be saved: as it is written, There shall come out of Sion the Deliverer, and shall turn away ungodliness from Jacob: For this is my covenant unto them, when I shall take away their sins.*

Here we have prophecy in the New Testament and we have prophecy that we have just read from Zechariah in the Old Testament.

In our study of Revelation, up to this point, we have had two phases of Christians being lifted from the earth. I believe there will be a few people, as a result of all the things that happen, who will acknowledge the Lord after the second lifting. They will go into the more intensified tribulation. It gets worse as time goes on.

We have to bear in mind that the "seven years" of tribulation is the last "week of years" of Israel's trouble prophesied in the twelfth chapter of Daniel.

The biggest argument I have heard against the eleventh chapter of Romans is: "Those people will not deserve to be saved." If someone makes up their mind to accept the Lord Jesus Christ, who are we to say they do not deserve to be saved? What has God done to help us make up our mind? He has done everything. We have all the influence God has given, all the revelation He has given, and still there is a world full of people who are putting their faith and trust in mankind and the riches of this world.

God will give power to the two olive trees. These are two individuals that are very much used of God…not only in this situation, but they have always been. They are God fearing men that have stood up for Him against the world. Who are the two olive trees? Let's see if the Bible gives us a clue. These two olive trees, two witnesses, the Bible tells us, will be expounding the Word of God to Israel. They will be doing this in the Holy Land.

As I said earlier, concerning Revelation, the world ruler will be a diplomatic individual. He will say I have something that will solve the world's problems. He will want peace. The Gentile world will sign a peace treaty with Israel, but not until Israel can have possession of the land they want. Hopefully, we will already be with God in heaven.

I want to point out that these two witnesses will arrive in Israel, from heaven, at the beginning of the tribulation period. After three and one-half years they will be lifted back up to heaven. Man will not have a weapon that will kill them. In other words, the smart bombs or whatever man may have will be rendered useless against them. The world will recognize them as being two individuals that they want removed from the earth, but God will protect them.

5. *And if any many will hurt them, fire proceedeth out of their mouth, and devoureth their enemies: and if any man will hurt them, he must in this manner be killed.* (The next verse identifies these two individuals).
6. *These have power to shut heaven, that it rain not in the days of their prophecy: and have power over waters to turn them to blood, and to smite the earth with all plagues, as often as they will.*

How can anyone say that the Bible does not identify these two? They had power when they were prophesying on this earth. Who had power to close heaven *that it rain not?* That is, unmistakably, Elijah. He called for it to *rain not* and it did not. He called for it to rain again and it did. Elijah is not the only one being talked about here. The other witness who had the power to turn water to blood and smite the earth with plagues is Moses. Here we have very distinct and clear identification of the two witnesses. They represent the Law and the Prophets. Who do we find conversing with Christ on the Mount of Transfiguration? The Holy Spirit said it was Moses and Elijah. They appeared with Christ and Peter identified them. He knew who they were.

Here again we find these two very important individuals. One of them never died as far as we know. He was called up into heaven in sight of the one that was to take his place. Man did not bury Moses. The Bible says he died and God buried him.

These two important individuals will witness to the Israelite people. They will witness to them about their Savior, the Savior that was one of them. Jesus said, *I came unto my own and my own received me not.* They reject Jesus, but these two witnesses will be preaching Jesus. They will tell them, "The one you rejected is your Savior." They will not try to force them to accept Jesus Christ, but will simply preach the message to them. As best I can tell they will not have a convert after three and one-half years of preaching. Someone may say, "It sounds like they will not be successful." God will not be using miraculous powers, but He will try to persuade. Sometimes the message of God is not popular with people. The message of God from these two individuals is not going to be popular with Israel, but it will be necessary that they hear it.

7. *And when they shall have finished their testimony, the beast that ascendeth out of the bottomless pit shall make war against them, and shall overcome them, and kill them.*

The two witnesses will overcome anyone that tries to harm them, but the beast that comes out of the bottomless pit (the spirit of Satan) will be able to kill them when the three and one-half years have ended.

8. And their dead bodies shall lie in the street of the great city, which spiritually is called Sodom and Egypt, where also our Lord was crucified.

The great city – always the Biblical name for Jerusalem is the *great city*. They will be killed in the street of the great city Jerusalem where our Lord was crucified.

9. And they of the people and kindreds and tongues and nations shall see their dead bodies three days and an half, and shall not suffer their dead bodies to be put in graves.

I can almost hear the world leader (first beast) when he is able to over-power these two witnesses: "Don't touch them, let them lay there! This will show the world that I have the power!" Can you imagine how they will gloat after not being able to kill these two witnesses for three and one-half years? This might have been impossible to interpret thirty years ago, but not now. By satellite television you can pick any spot on this earth and show it to the whole world. They will be able to show the dead bodies of these two witnesses continuously on television.

10. And they that dwell upon the earth shall rejoice over them, and make merry, and shall send gifts one to another; because these two prophets tormented them that dwelt on the earth.

They will send gifts and have parties all over the earth to celebrate the killing of these two witnesses.

11. And after three days and an half the Spirit of life from God entered into them, and they stood upon their feet; and great fear fell upon them which saw them.

> *12. And they heard a great voice from heaven saying unto them, Come up hither. And they ascended up to heaven in a cloud; and their enemies beheld them.*

God will show the world how powerful He is. The two witnesses that have been dead for three and one-half days will stand up and show the whole world that they are alive. That will serve quite a blow to the world leader. God is going to show everyone that they are alive. As the world watches, the two witnesses will begin to lift from the earth. Remember Jesus as the disciples watched and gazed into the sky? He just simply disappeared. At the lifting of Jesus, friends were watching, but as the two witnesses ascend up to heaven, the enemy will be watching.

> *13. And the same hour was there a great earthquake, and the tenth part of the city fell, and in the earthquake were slain of men seven thousand; and the remnant were affrighted, and gave glory to the God of heaven.*

Immediately the earthquake will take place and seeing the people that are slain will cause the nation of Israel in and around Jerusalem to accept the Lord Jesus Christ. They will remember what the two witnesses told them. Ungodliness will be turned away from the house of Jacob.

This answers the question in the eleventh chapter of Romans where *blindness has come to them in part,* so we can once again read that chapter and know something about what it says.

The prophecy in the book of Revelation interprets the Old Testament and New Testament prophecy concerning Israel.

14. *The second woe is past; and, behold, the third woe cometh quickly.*

15. *And the seventh angel sounded; and there were great voices in heaven, saying, The kingdoms of this world are become the kingdoms of our Lord, and of his Christ; and he shall reign for ever and ever.*

16. *And the four and twenty elders, which sat before God on their seats, fell upon their faces, and worshipped God,*

17. *Saying, We give thee thanks, O Lord God Almighty, which art, and wast, and art to come; because thou hast taken to thee thy great power, and hast reigned.*

18. *And the nations were angry, and thy wrath is come, and the time of the dead, that they should be judged, and that thou shouldest give reward unto thy servants the prophets, and to the saints, and them that fear thy name, small and great; and shouldest destroy them which destroy the earth.*

19. *And the temple of God was opened in heaven, and there was seen in his temple the ark of his testament; and there were lightnings, and voices, and thunderings, and an earthquake, and great hail.*

Here we have a preview of what is about to take place.

We have seen previews where excerpts have been taken from throughout a movie. I am sure an individual who is inspired to write the story for a movie has an overview of it and then he writes.

God is allowing us to see something here like an overview of His mind – as to what is taking place. He knows what is going to happen. He already has it figured out.

If we start to construct a building and it is a perfectly still day, perfect for a month, weather wise, we might say, "I won't need bracing in this building because of this great, still, weather." As an overview in our mind, before we ever start that building and even though we have had a month of perfect weather, we say, "I have got to make this building strong because eventually the storms will come. I cannot prepare it to stand for only one month."

God knows the storms are coming. God knows that Satan is alive and is His enemy just like we know that the winds will rage. Well, Satan will rage against God's plan to save His people.

CHAPTER 12

1. And there appeared a great wonder in heaven; a woman clothed with the sun, and the moon under her feet, and upon her head a crown of twelve stars:

The woman mentioned here is the nation of Israel.
God knows that Satan is going to do everything he can to keep people from being saved...to keep people from returning to Him.

God said, "I will prepare a nation." As you study your Bible, did He not do that – did He not begin to do that with Abraham and continue all the way through? God did not take away their freedom of choice even though He sometimes felt like destroying them. Moses and Abraham interceded with the anger of God when He felt like destroying them all. That proves He did not take away their freedom of will, but He prepared a nation to bring the Savior into the world. This nation was the initial source of Light to the world. We must let the Light of Jesus shine through us. We are not the source of the Light, but we are the reflectors of the Light.

*...and upon her head a crown of twelve stars...*These twelve stars represent the twelve tribes of Israel.

2. And she being with child cried, travailing in birth, and pained to be delivered.

3. *And there appeared another wonder in heaven; and behold a great red dragon, having seven heads and ten horns, and seven crowns upon his heads.*

4. *And his tail drew the third part of the stars of heaven, and did cast them to the earth: and the dragon stood before the woman which was ready to be delivered, for to devour her child as soon as it was born.*

5. *And she brought forth a man-child, who was to rule all nations with a rod of iron: and her child was caught up unto God, and to His throne.*

The man-child here is no doubt Jesus Christ. Mary, as a citizen of Israel, would not only draw Satan's wrath to her, but to the whole nation.

Satan wants mankind to be in the same boat he is in. He knows that his time is short – that he is destined for eternal punishment. I cannot tell you why Satan has the leverage that he has today. But we know he has limited power. What happened to put Satan in the position he is in? The Bible tells us that he rebelled against God.

...and her child was caught up unto God, and to his throne. Jesus ascended into heaven and sits on the right-hand of God.

6. *And the woman fled into the wilderness, where she hath a place prepared of God, that they should feed her there a thousand two hundred and threescore days.*

Satan will make war with the nation and they will flee their land. They will turn to God and accept Jesus Christ.

There is an ecumenical movement that wants to accept every belief. There is only one belief that will save us...the one based on the Word of God.

I heard a leader of the Christian Coalition of America say that the Western world needs a new Bible – one that all can agree on. If you think that is not dangerous, think again. Sometimes I may not like to discipline myself according to God's Holy Word, but I have found that it is very comforting to do what God says. It is the only safety on this earth. We do not need a new Bible!

God tells us here of a war that took place in heaven.

> 7. *And there was a war in heaven: Michael and his angels fought against the dragon; and the dragon fought and his angels,*
> 8. *And prevailed not; neither was their place found any more in heaven.*
> 9. *And the great dragon was cast out, that old serpent, called the Devil, and Satan, which deceiveth the whole world: he was cast out into the earth, and his angels were cast out with him.*
> 10. *And I heard a loud voice saying in heaven, Now is come salvation, and strength, and the kingdom of our God, and the power of his Christ: for the accuser of our brethren is cast down, which accused them before our God day and night.*
> 11. *And they overcame him by the blood of the Lamb, and by the word of their testimony; and they loved not their lives unto the death.*

The blood of the Lamb has defeated Satan. His plan has been spoiled by God's great plan of redemption. God's plan includes the patriarchs of the Bible, the nation of Israel, and a family from the nation of Israel. That is why Satan hates this nation. Now he is basking in glee over their rejection of Christ. He will not like the things that start to happen in the end time.

The people who have been obedient to the blood of the Lamb *loved not their lives unto death.* The apostles were

willing to die for the cause. In the Fox's Book of Martyrs we
find that seven million people died for the cause.

> 12. *Therefore rejoice, ye heavens, and ye that dwell in
> them. Woe to the inhabiters of the earth and of the
> sea! For the devil is come down unto you, having
> great wrath, because he knoweth that he hath but a
> short time.*
> 13. *And when the dragon saw that he was cast unto the
> earth, he persecuted the woman which brought forth
> the man-child.*

The woman is the nation of Israel. Satan (the dragon)
persecuted the woman that brought forth the man-child.

> 14. *And to the woman were given two wings of a great
> eagle, that she might fly into the wilderness, into her
> place, where she is nourished for a time, and times,
> and half a time, from the face of a serpent.*

At the end time the nation is driven out of her land. The
world leader will break the treaty that was signed with Israel.
They will go into hiding and be protected by God.

> 15. *And the serpent cast out of his mouth water as a
> flood after the woman, that he might cause her to be
> carried away of the flood.*
> 16. *And the earth helped the woman, and the earth
> opened her mouth, and swallowed up the flood which
> the dragon cast out of his mouth.*

We know that the earth can absorb a lot of destruction
and it can be a lot of protection.

Do you remember when everyone was afraid that
communist Russia might start a nuclear war? We knew that

we had to have so many feet of earth above us, some sort of protective den in the earth. We were told that this was the best protection we could have. Many people still have those shelters that were built years ago.

I am not going to speculate and tell you that I know what the world leader will be able to do against the nation of Israel (the woman), but they will take refuge and be protected by the earth.

> *17. And the dragon was wroth with the woman, and went to make war with the remnant of her seed, which keep the commandments of God, and have the testimony of Jesus Christ.*

The dragon (Satan) will be angry with the woman (nation of Israel) and will make war with the remnant of her seed (those who will be living).

There is no scripture indicating that unconverted Jews will be resurrected from the grave. When we die, our destination is sealed, whether Jew or Gentile.

Premillennialism comes in all forms and fashions. Don't ever lump them all together. I have heard of many different beliefs being called premillennialism. Seeing what the Bible has to say puts a lot of them in the category of no scriptural support.

The Jews will not be brought back to life and given a second chance to accept Jesus Christ. The remnant of the seed is what is being talked about here – the ones that survive and by their own free will, accept Jesus Christ as their Savior.

As we continue with the preview of what is to come…

CHAPTER 13

1. And I stood upon the sand of the sea, and saw a beast rise up out of the sea, having seven heads and ten horns, and upon his horns ten crowns, and upon his heads the name of blasphemy.

The beast to rise out of the sea (of people) will be the world leader who is seeking power and backing from the rest of the world. Many nations will give their support. He will be the world power.

2. And the beast which I saw was like unto a leopard, and his feet were as the feet of a bear, and his mouth as the mouth of a lion: and the dragon gave him his power, and his seat, and great authority.

The world leader (first beast) will get his inspiration from Satan (the dragon). We know that the apostles of Jesus were Holy Spirit inspired and we know that all scripture was Holy Spirit inspired. We have Godly inspiration and we have Satanic inspiration in the world. That is why there is terrible danger in saying, "I do not have scriptural support for this, but I believe it in my heart." You may believe it in your heart and be right, but you may believe it in your heart and be wrong if you do not have Bible to back your belief.

3. And I saw one of his heads as it were wounded to death; and his deadly wound was healed: and all the world wondered after the beast.

Why will they wonder after him? The beast will have a deadly wound – he will be assassinated. Satan performs a miracle and the world leader with the deadly wound will be healed. Satan (the dragon) will duplicate the resurrection of Jesus Christ. Can you imagine a world ruler being assassinated and then resurrected? He was, was not, and was again – that is what the Bible says. There will be miracles and wonders that will blaspheme God. Can you imagine the confusion in the world? No wonder the Bible says that even the very elect will be deceived.

4. And they worshipped the dragon which gave power unto the beast: and they worshipped the beast, saying, Who is like unto the beast? who is able to make war with him?

5. And there was given unto him a mouth speaking great things and blasphemies; and power was given unto him to continue forty and two months.

He will rule and have power for forty-two months...three and one-half years.

6. And he opened his mouth in blasphemy against God, to blaspheme his name and his tabernacle, and them that dwell in heaven.

The world leader will claim to be God himself.

7. And it was given unto him to make war with the saints, and to overcome them: and power was given him over all kindreds, and tongues, and nations.

8. *And all that dwell upon the earth shall worship him,
whose names are not written in the book of life of the
Lamb slain from the foundation of the world.*

9. *If any man have an ear, let him hear.*

10. *He that leadeth into captivity shall go into captivity:
he that killeth with the sword must be killed with
the sword. Here is the patience and the faith of the
saints.*

Satan does not have power to do miracles unless God
allows him to do so, such as in the case of Job's testing.
These people who were deceived by the miracles of Satan
had been deceived already. They had blasphemed God, His
power and His Word.

Do you remember what Paul said? ...*He led captivity
captive and gave gifts to men.* Sin captivated man. Jesus led
captivity captive and gave gifts to men to preach the gospel
to the world. We can now lead people who are captivated by
sin to freedom.

11. *And I beheld another beast coming up out of the earth;
and he had two horns like a lamb, and he spake as a
dragon.*

Who is this character? He will have all the clergy
credentials. He will be a graduate of the very best religious
schools.

We have to stay sharp on the Word of God, otherwise,
how can we recognize false teaching? How will we know if
a preacher or teacher is telling the Truth?

We are incurably religious. We are, by nature, spiritual
beings. We may not always pursue the Truth, but we, as
human beings, want to believe there is a greater power. That
is the way God made us.

The world leader (first beast) sees that he cannot fulfill the spiritual nature of man. When he realizes he cannot do this he will use a false prophet. The false prophet (second beast) will have two horns like a lamb, but he will not speak like a lamb. He will speak like a dragon. He will be inspired of Satan. He will tell the people, however, that he is spiritual and will fulfill all spiritual needs. For this reason Satan (the dragon) and the world leader (first beast) share power with him.

12. *And he exerciseth all the power of the first beast before him, and causeth the earth and them which dwell therein to worship the first beast, whose deadly wound was healed.*

He will exercise the same power as the first beast. Look what we have now – three as one. We now see a false prophet and a world leader and we see both of them getting their power from Satan. But if they say they are getting their power from Satan they cannot fool anyone. That is not what they will say. The Holy Spirit is making us wise because we are studying His Word, but these people will not know God's Word and will not be wise.

13. *And he doeth great wonders, so that he maketh fire come down from heaven on the earth in the sight of men.*

Does God do every miracle? Or does Satan also do miracles? He does, I'm sorry to say…and they are not all bad. If he only did bad miracles he could not fool people.

14. *And deceiveth them that dwell on the earth, by the means of those miracles which he had power to do in the sight of the beast; saying to them that dwell on the*

*earth, that they should make an image to the beast,
which had the wound by a sword, and did live.*

The false prophet will deceive people into thinking that
he is a true prophet of God.

In verse 14 he says, "What we need to do now is make
an image of this man (the world leader). We will make something that looks like him in the form of a statue." He wants
to impress the world leader. They will make an image of the
(first) beast.

There is nothing wrong in making an image of someone
as long as we do not worship it. It is not uncommon that
power-seeking individuals want to be worshipped. The
Roman Emperors wanted the world to worship them. In
the Old Testament we find that prophets of God refused to
worship worldly images.

*15. And he had power to give life unto the image of the
beast, that the image of the beast should both speak,
and cause that as many as would not worship the
image of the beast should be killed.*

The false prophet (second beast) will have power (from
Satan) to give life to the image of the world leader. At this
point we have evidence of another evil spirit on the scene.
The image will speak and will have everyone killed that
does not worship him. So many people will be deceived. It
will be a bad time to live on this earth. Keep in mind the
world leader and the false prophet. It is important that we
remember these three as we go on through the balance of
this chapter. Anyone who will not worship the image will be
killed. I think it is Satan that will speak through the image.

Bear in mind that Jesus Christ came to this earth and
He said, "If you know me, you know my Father. I can only

speak the will of my Father. The power that I have, He gives me."

We are about to see a counterfeit of the Trinity. We know that the Father, Son, and Holy Spirit created and sustain this world. We know that all goodness, love, and mercy come from Them. The opposite will come from Satan (dragon) in the form of the image, the world leader (first beast), and the false prophet (second beast).

> *16. And he causeth all, both small and great, rich and poor, free and bond, to receive a mark in their right hand, or in their foreheads:*
> *17. And that no man might buy or sell, save he that had the mark or the name of the beast, or the number of his name.*

Many people are afraid of the numbers 6-6-6. I don't like them either. However, the number six has some significance for us. I read in the Bible that six is the number of man. If six is the number of man, then that is what we are. We are sixes. What significance is the "six?"

There are a lot of sevens in the Bible. Sevens are pretty significant in the book of Revelation. Seven means a lot when we think of what <u>we</u> are in regards to God. He created man to be an intelligent human being. God created man to be pretty powerful, but He did not create him to be more powerful than He is. The Father, Son, and Holy Spirit is a Seven. God created all living creatures, but only man is a six. God says in His Word that Satan is a created being. He developed himself to be anti-God. He is a fallen angel that can enter the body of man and speak through him. The Bible tells us that he made war against God and drew off a large portion of the population of heaven. Those followers are still helping him.

18. Here is wisdom: Let him that hath understanding count the number of the beast: for it is the number of a man; and his number is Six hundred threescore and six.

As the dragon, world leader, and false prophet work together **as one** they will select a number that will identify their leadership to the world. The Bible says the Father, Son, and Holy Spirit are **as One.**

We must remember that God has said He will put Satan (the dragon) where he can tempt man no more. I believe He will do that and I look forward to the day.

...*Six hundred threescore and six*...the three individuals, the dragon, world leader, and false prophet will be three **as one.** If the dragon says do it, it will be done. If the world leader tells the people to do something, it will be approved of the dragon. The false prophet will carry out the will of the dragon.

The number they choose that will be required to buy or sell may not be 6-6-6. The 6-6-6 in the Bible identifies the three leaders as men.

The world now has equipment to read numbers on or under your skin that are not visible to the eye. There is enough technology now to accomplish the things prophesied for the end times. Can you imagine going in to buy your groceries and having your hand or head scanned? If you take the number of the beast it will be irreversible. No one can go to the doctor or take their children to the doctor without the mark of the beast. I doubt there will be many young children alive at that time. Those under the age of accountability will be in the hands of God.

This is a very controversial and crucial part of studying the book of Revelation.

CHAPTER 14

1. *And I looked, and lo, a Lamb stood on the mount Sion, and with him an hundred forty and four thousand, having his Father's name written in their foreheads.*
2. *And I heard a voice from heaven, as the voice of many waters, and as the voice of a great thunder: and I heard the voice of harpers harping with their harps:*
3. *And they sung as it were a new song before the throne, and before the four beasts, and the elders: and no man could learn that song but the hundred and forty four thousand, which were redeemed from the earth.*

Don't forget the word "were" – were redeemed from the earth.

I have not met many people, who have studied this, that do not try to put this hundred and forty four thousand back on the earth. If you put this group back on the earth, you are putting them somewhere that God does not put them. This group will be included in the first lifting of Christians from the earth. I have heard many people say that this group of one hundred and forty four thousand is the same as the first group mentioned (Revelation 7:4-8). Just because it is the same number does not mean it is the same group. Go back and read about the two celebrations in heaven (Rev. 4:1-3 and Rev. 7:9-13) and you will see that this celebration sounds exactly like the one in Revelation 4:1-3, but they are a selected group from the first lifting of Christians (Revelation 4) from the earth.

*...before the four beasts...*The Holy Spirit has used the same word here that is used for powerful individuals of Satan, but these four beasts are powerful individuals of God. *And they sung as it were a new song before the throne, and before the four beasts, and the elders:...*They are not called twenty-four elders here, but they are in other scripture. No man can learn that song but the hundred and forty four thousand.

The fourth verse tells us who they are.

> 4. *These are they which were not defiled with women; for they are virgins. These are they which follow the Lamb whithersoever he goeth. These were redeemed from among men, being the firstfruits unto God and to the Lamb.*

These are they which were not defiled with women; In Hebrews13:4 it reads: *Marriage is honourable in all, and the bed undefiled: but whoremongers and adulterers God will judge.*

Within the bounds of Holy Matrimony men are not defiled with women. The Bible says so.

These will have been redeemed from the earth, so that puts them out of the category of being <u>on</u> the earth.

The Bible also tells us, in Romans 8:23, some of who will be included in this group: *And not only they, but ourselves also, which have the first fruits of the Spirit, even we ourselves groan within ourselves, waiting for the adoption, to wit, the redemption of our body.*

Let's further identify the firstfruits:

James 1:18 *Of his own will begat he us with the word of the truth, that we should be a kind of firstfruits of his creatures.*

This James was not an apostle, but he includes himself in the *firstfruits*, so this means we have to spread out the *firstfruits*. We have to go farther than the apostles. I do not think it will include the patriarchs or the twelve tribes, but this group begins with the apostles. How could we miss the fact that the Bible says they are a part of the *firstfruits*? The church had its beginning in the book of Acts and the *firstfruits* mentioned were the apostles.

We have one hundred and forty four thousand following the Lamb – never defiled themselves on the earth.

5. *And in their mouth was found no guile: for they are without fault before the throne of God.*

This does not mean they never committed a sin, but that as they repented, the blood of the Lamb covered their sins.

We have a responsibility as Christians to preach the gospel to every creature on this earth.

Every time I say that, I am reminded of a black Christian Church preacher whose name was Brother Moore. He lived during slave times and during those slave years a lot of people thought blacks were not human. Every time he said anything in his sermon about the creatures he would say, "We may not be human, but we are creatures." I do not agree with the statement that they may not be human. They are human.

The Supreme Court of the United States once ruled that blacks were not human. That goes to prove that the Supreme Court is not always right.

As a royal priesthood we are to preach the gospel to every creature. We cannot hire someone to do that for us. We cannot hire a preacher to spread the gospel for us. He can do that for himself, but he cannot do it for us. He cannot call on the sick for us – we have to do that ourselves. There is going to be a judgment day. Our preacher will be judged on what he should have done, and I will be judged on what I should have done. God is in the process of judging the world right now. We will be judged not only by what we already know, but also by what is available for us to know.

We do not have special gifts today that would enable us to know sound doctrine. We must study the written Word. Developing spiritually is a slow process. We have to study and be willing to apply ourselves to what we learn from the Bible.

We cannot grow in Spirit and in Truth until we are willing to do what God says. As Christians we have a peace of mind that only God can give. As Christians we have the strength to withstand the storms of life. If you are not a Christian, you do not have the peace that passes all understanding, but it is available to you. To have that peace you must subscribe to it according to God's Word.

> 6. *And I saw another angel fly in the midst of heaven, having the everlasting gospel to preach unto them that dwell on the earth, and to every nation, and kindred, and tongue, and people,*

In this verse we see the earth populated with people that are practically illiterate, spiritually, but they are people that God created and He loves them. He has an angel to preach the gospel to them. This could indicate that there are no Christians left, knowledgeable enough of God's Word, to preach the gospel. Since Matthew 28, man has been commissioned to preach the gospel, but we see here that God will approve this change for the sake of His righteous judgment.

> 7. *Saying with a loud voice, Fear God, and give glory to him; for the hour of his judgment is come: and worship him that made heaven, and earth, and the sea, and the fountains of waters.*

This is the message of the angel preaching with a loud voice to every nation on the earth. How God will accomplish this I do not know. He will be watching, waiting, longing and hoping that they submit to Him and His Word.

8. *And there followed another angel, saying, Babylon is fallen, is fallen, that great city, because she made all nations drink of the wine of the wrath of her fornication.*
9. *And the third angel followed them, saying with a loud voice, If any man worship the beast and his image, and receive his mark in his forehead, or in his hand,*
10. *The same shall drink of the wine of the wrath of God, which is poured out without mixture into the cup of his indignation; and he shall be tormented with fire and brimstone in the presence of the holy angels, and in the presence of the Lamb;*

Here we find the wrath of God, without mixture. In other words, it will not be diluted, but will be the full wrath of God.

As Lot and his family left the city of Sodom, God warned them to not look back.

In this verse, God gives a warning of what will happen to the people that reject Him. There will be no more mercy extended. God's mercy will come to an end. These people who continually reject Him and take the mark of the beast will be tormented in the presence of the angels and the Lamb.

11. *And the smoke of their torment ascendth up for ever and ever: and they have no rest day nor night, who worship the beast and his image, and whosoever receiveth the mark of his name.*
12. *Here is the patience of the saints: here are they that keep the commandments of God, and the faith of Jesus.*

*13. And I heard a voice from heaven saying unto me,
Write, Blessed are the dead which die in the Lord
from henceforth: Yea, saith the Spirit, that they may
rest from their labours; and their works do follow
them.*

God has told what will happen to those who reject Him,
but He also has something to say here in regards to those
who accept Him.

This is a very famous passage of scripture at funerals. It
is one of the most comforting messages that can be found in
the Bible.

The time we spend for the Lord is not wasted. Anything
we do for the Lord will not go unnoticed. Every little thing
will be remembered.

*14. And I looked, and behold a white cloud, and upon
the cloud one sat like unto the Son of man, having
on his head a golden crown, and in his hand a sharp
sickle.*

As we study through the remaining part of this chapter,
the Holy Spirit is allowing us to see and know what is going
to take place. This is an overview of what is about to happen
– the harvest of the earth. We have to remember, as we study
in the book of Revelation, that the things being talked about
may not be happening at the very moment, but may be future
happenings. This is what is at hand.

*15. And another angel came out of the temple, crying
with a loud voice to him that sat on the cloud, Thrust
in thy sickle, and reap: for the time is come for thee
to reap; for the harvest of the earth is ripe.*
*16. And he that sat on the cloud thrust in his sickle on the
earth; and the earth was reaped.*

This will be the beginning of reaping the harvest from the earth. The Bible tells us that the chaff will be gathered and burned (this is mentioned in other places of the Bible).

This world has not always had combines. In my grandparents day the only harvesting done was with a sickle. I remember seeing the old sickle with five wooden fingers on it. The men would cut and catch the grain, tie it into bundles, and then separate the chaff from the grain by machine. The sickle is always associated with *harvest*.

17. *And another angel came out of the temple which is in heaven, he also having a sharp sickle.*
18. *And another angel came out from the altar, which had power over fire; and cried with a loud cry to him that had the sharp sickle, saying, Thrust in thy sharp sickle, and gather the clusters of the vine of the earth; for her grapes are fully ripe.*

Satan and his influence is about to come to an end.

We have always known that this system is not going to last forever, but it is not popular to talk about the end time.

When I was a young boy I remember hearing my Dad say, "I think we are living in the last days." I thought, "Why does he always say that?" But I realize now that it is not a good idea to think the end will not come. God's timetable will reach its limit.

19. *And the angel thrust in his sickle into the earth, and gathered the vine of the earth, and cast it into the great winepress of the wrath of God.*
20. *And the winepress was trodden without the city, and blood came out of the winepress, even unto the horse bridles, by the space of a thousand and six hundred furlongs.*

I have heard that some people today are watching for a war to break out in the Middle East that will escalate into the final war. I think they are wrong because this battle is going to be controlled by God, not man. Predictions such as that should be taken with a grain of salt – they are not scriptural.

According to the King James translation, a thousand and six hundred furlongs is two hundred miles.

The people dedicated to the dragon, world leader, and false prophet, will sacrifice their eternal life with God out of dedication to the evil government. That evil system will lose the war. Their blood will run as deep as the horse's bridle, for 200 miles.

CHAPTER 15

1. And I saw another sign in heaven, great and marvelous, seven angels having the seven last plagues; for in them is filled up the wrath of God.

These seven angels will be carrying out the last seven plagues. What are the plagues? They are the various things that will happen on the earth and will be controlled by the seven angels.

2. And I saw as it were a sea of glass mingled with fire: and them that had gotten the victory over the beast, and over his image, and over his mark, and over the number of his name, stand on the sea of glass, having the harps of God.
3. And they sing the song of Moses the servant of God, and the song of the Lamb, saying, Great and marvelous are thy works, Lord God Almighty; just and true are thy ways, thou King of saints.

This is referring to the song of Moses, found in Exodus 15:1-18. He led the Israelites to freedom as they crossed through the parted waters of the Red Sea. This is the song they will sing – the song of Moses.

This verse is talking about those who will have already been victorious. This is the converted remnant of the nation of Israel referred to in the eleventh chapter of Revelation. They will be victorious because they will overcome their unbelief and accept Jesus Christ as their Savior. We see the remnant of this nation that will stand up for God, and in the second verse we see they are standing on a sea of glass, meaning safety and peace. A sea of glass is smooth – no waves. The sea is peaceful. They are at peace now. They sing the song of Moses and they have another song to sing – the song of the Lamb, which is Jesus Christ, victorious.

4. *Who shall not fear thee, O Lord, and glorify thy name? For thou only art holy: for all nations shall come and worship before thee; for thy judgments are made manifest.*
5. *And after that I looked, and, behold, the temple of the tabernacle of the testimony in heaven was opened:*
6. *And the seven angels came out of the temple, having the seven plagues, clothed in pure and white linen, and having their breasts girded with golden girdles.*
7. *And one of the four beasts gave unto the seven angels seven golden vials full of the wrath of God, who liveth for ever and ever.*

These seven angels will be chosen to pour out the last seven plagues upon the people of the earth.

8. *And the temple was filled with smoke from the glory of God, and from his power; and no man was able to enter into the temple, till the seven plagues of the seven angels were fulfilled.*

The authority for the seven angels to bring about the plagues will come from the temple of God. This does not mean a building on earth, but in heaven. When we think of the temple of God, we know that Jesus is sitting at His right hand in the judgment seat.

The smoke signifies the glory of God. No one can enter the temple until the seven plagues are fulfilled. They will produce the bloodshed of man on the earth that will run for 200 miles. This will be an end to the prince of this world – Satan, the world leader, and the false prophet. That is the kind of battle it will be.

When we think of this number fighting against the Almighty God it is hard for us to imagine the magnitude of suffering that will take place in this war. It will be the last battle. It will be instigated of Satan, but God will be in control.

CHAPTER 16

1. And I heard a great voice out of the temple saying to the seven angels, Go your ways, and pour out the vials of the wrath of God upon the earth.

I think there will probably be a few individuals that turn to God during this time, but they will have to stay in hiding. That is why I say there will be people living off the land, but they cannot buy or sell.

The plagues will be punishment upon the people who reject the One True God.

It is going to be one of the most confusing times on earth because Satan, the world leader, and the false prophet will identify themselves as angels of light. They are going to say, "We will take care of you."

The new world system will be coming to a close, as we find the seven angels going out to deliver punishment upon people who take the mark of the beast.

2. And the first went, and poured out his vial upon the earth; and there fell a noisome and grievous sore upon the men which had the mark of the beast, and upon them which worshipped his image.

We read earlier about the false prophet making an image of the world leader and the image being able to speak.

> *3. And the second angel poured out his vial upon the sea; and it became as the blood of a dead man: and every living soul died in the sea.*
> *4. And the third angel poured out his vial upon the rivers and fountains of waters; and they became blood.*

The second angel will effect the seas and the third angel will pollute the rivers and underground water source – *and they became blood.*

> *5. And I heard the angel of the waters say, Thou art righteous, O Lord, which art, and wast, and shalt be, because thou hast judged thus.*
> *6. For they have shed the blood of saints and prophets, and thou hast given them blood to drink; for they are worthy.*
> *7. And I heard another out of the altar say, Even so, Lord God Almighty, true and righteous are thy judgments.*

God's powerful caretaker of the world's water approves God's judgment.

In verse 6, the angel is saying: "the wicked people that killed the prophets and the saints of God are getting what they deserve."

Some people say that we, who are sinners, killed Christ. I am thankful that Christ came. I could not get forgiveness of my sins and have the hope of eternal life if He had not come to this earth and shed His blood for me. In that sense, I can say I am glad Jesus came and suffered. It makes me feel sad to say that, but I have to say it…we all do. That does not make the people that killed Him any less guilty.

John hears approval from heaven. God is doing these things against the system that killed His prophets and His Son – the system that rejects His Word. It is a serious thing to reject the Word of God.

> *8. And the fourth angel poured out his vial upon the sun; and power was given unto him to scorch men with fire.*

We know there are certain times in the year that the sun is so hot we can hardly stand it, but this doesn't even compare to what will be happening then.

> *9. And men were scorched with great heat, and blasphemed the name of God, which hath power over these plagues: and they repented not to give him glory.*

The people who take the mark of the beast will know that God is doing this, but they will blaspheme Him and deny that He has power over the beast and the false prophet.

> *10. And the fifth angel poured out his vial upon the seat of the beast; and his kingdom was full of darkness; and they gnawed their tongues for pain,*

The fifth angel affects the city where the world ruler has his headquarters.

> *11. And blasphemed the God of heaven because of their pains and their sores, and repented not of their deeds.*

Again, we find them recognizing that they have no power to stop these things.

12. *And the sixth angel poured out his vial upon the great river Euphrates and the water thereof was dried up, that the way of the kings of the east might be prepared.*

The sixth angel will dry up the river Euphrates. The Garden of Eden, as we see in the Bible, was in this region. I think the final battle against sin will be won in the same place where sin started. Of course God is going to be victorious, but this is significant in that the river Euphrates will be dried up to prepare a more convenient place for this great battle.

13. *And I saw three unclean spirits like frogs come out of the mouth of the dragon, and out of the mouth of the beast, and out of the mouth of the false prophet.*
14. *For they are the spirits of devils, working miracles, which go forth unto the kings of the earth and of the whole world, to gather them to the battle of that great day of God Almighty.*

The dragon, beast, and false prophet will give instructions to the whole world.

15. *Behold, I come as a thief. Blessed is he that watcheth, and keepeth his garments, lest he walk naked, and they see his shame.*

Christ's coming will be unexpected by Satan and his followers. Jesus said, in Matthew 25:13...*keep watch, because you do not know the day or the hour.*

In I Thessalonians 5:4, Paul, speaking to Christians, says, *But ye, brethren, are not in darkness, that that day should overtake you as a thief.*

*16. And he gathered them together into a place called in
the Hebrew tongue Armageddon.*

This is where the great battle will be fought.

*17. And the seventh angel poured out his vial into the
air; and there came a great voice out of the temple of
heaven, from the throne, saying, It is done.*

*18. And there were voices, and thunders, and lightnings;
and there was a great earthquake, such as was not
since men were upon the earth, so mighty an earthquake, and so great.*

*19. And the great city was divided into three parts, and
the cities of the nations fell: and great Babylon came
in remembrance before God, to give unto her the cup
of the wine of the fierceness of his wrath.*

The Jews will be driven out of the city. It will be taken
over as headquarters of Satan (dragon), the world leader
(first beast) and the false prophet (second beast). The great
city will be divided into three parts.

*20. And every island fled away, and the mountains were
not found.*

This is the beginning of a re-shaping of the earth. Can
you imagine the difference it will make when the mountains
are leveled and the valleys filled up?

We are using only one-fifth of the earth's surface. The
rest of it is swamp, rivers, wasteland, and oceans.

This will make the entire surface of the earth usable.

*21. And there fell upon men a great hail out of heaven,
every stone about the weight of a talent: and men*

blasphemed God because of the plague of the hail;
for the plague thereof was exceeding great.

Once, I almost got into trouble over this because I gave the wrong weight. The King James translation and the NIV say one hundred pounds. A fifty-pound stone can do about as much damage as a hundred-pound stone and one hundred pounds can do about as much damage as a ton. We know that it will be a very destructive force.

CHAPTER 17

1. And there came one of the seven angels which had the seven vials, and talked with me, saying unto me, Come hither; I will shew unto thee the judgment of the great whore that sitteth upon many waters.

This is still a preview that John is able to see before it actually happens.

The whore, referred to in this verse, is the false religious system that has deceived the people of the earth and continues to do so.

In Hosea, first and second chapters, we find that God told Hosea to marry a woman of whoredom and have children. God said this is what Israel is doing to me. He said they are whoring after other gods and listening to instructions that I do not sanction. Bear in mind that during this time they were still supporting the temple of God. They were going through a formality of worshipping the One True God.

When we read of whoredom in the Bible, it means false religion...not approved by the God of heaven.

2. With whom the kings of the earth have committed fornication, and the inhabitants of the earth have been made drunk with the wine of her fornication.

3. So he carried me away in the spirit into the wilderness: and I saw a woman sit upon a scarlet coloured beast, full of names of blasphemy, having seven heads and ten horns.

4. And the woman was arrayed in purple and scarlet colour, and decked with gold and previous stones and pearls, having a golden cup in her hand full of abominations and filthiness of her fornication:

5. And upon her forehead was a name written, MYSTERY, BABYLON THE GREAT, THE MOTHER OF HARLOTS AND ABOMINATIONS OF THE EARTH.

Today we see some of the finest buildings of worship. In the midst of poverty we find big cathedrals. It is not hard to see that some of the richest, most expensive structures are church buildings. We cannot help but see what God is talking about here.

When we ask some people if they believe the Bible is God's final Word and that it thoroughly furnishes us with instruction from God, we see a puzzled look.

People that are worshipping buildings, shrines, statues, gold and silver, or anything else, are not obeying God's Word.

6. And I saw the woman drunken with the blood of the saints, and with the blood of the martyrs of Jesus: and when I saw her, I wondered with great admiration.

The word "admiration" in the King James Bible is an incorrect translation from the original Greek. The NIV says, "I was greatly astonished." This is a better translation of the word.

When we check history, we find that the Israelite people rejected the word of God and went into apostasy (false religion). They killed the prophets of God and rejected and killed

Jesus Christ. The people that did those things were a part of the same system we have today. They decide what part of God's Word they will accept and what part they will reject.

The woman (false religious system) is drunk with the blood of the saints and with the blood of the prophets and Jesus. This has happened down through the history of time and will be happening in the end time.

> 7. *And the angel said unto me, Wherefore didst thou marvel? I will tell thee the mystery of the woman, and of the beast that carrieth her, which hath the seven heads and ten horns.*

John said he looked with great astonishment. The angel said, "Why do you marvel at that? I will tell you the mystery of the woman and the beast that carries her."

This verse is saying that the world leader is supporting the false prophet (head of the false religious system).

> 8. *The beast that thou sawest was, and is not; and shall ascend out of the bottomless pit, and go into perdition: and they that dwell on the earth shall wonder, whose names were not written in the book of life from the foundation of the world, when they behold the beast that was, and is not, and yet is.*

Remember the beast that was, and is not, and yet is? He will be assassinated and the dragon will bring him back to life...he is able to resurrect him.

Earlier in this study, the book of life was mentioned. Here we have it mentioned again. God enters the name of everyone that is conceived in the womb, into the book of life, from the foundation of the world.

Reasons for being blotted out of the book of life are:

- Anyone that has reached the age of accountability and dies without confessing Jesus Christ as Savior.
- Anyone who comes to know Christ as Lord and Savior, but grows cold and indifferent toward God and the Holy Spirit breathed Word *shall not be forgiven* (Matthew 12:31-32, Jude 5:6, I John 5:16-17), Hebrew 6:4 and 8). This is known as the unpardonable sin
- Anyone who takes away from the words of the book of this prophecy, which is Revelation (Rev. 22:19).
- Anyone that takes the mark of the beast in the end-time (this being irreversible) will have his or her name blotted out. In the eighth verse it says...*whose names were not written in the book of life*. Those who take the number of the beast will not be found in the book of life.

9. *And here is the mind which hath wisdom. The seven heads are seven mountains, on which the woman sitteth.*

We have already established that the woman mentioned here is referring to false religion in the world. The *seven mountains*, in this verse, are seven world powers.

10. *And there are seven kings: five are fallen, and one is, and the other is not yet come; and when he cometh, he must continue a short space.*
11. *And the beast that was, and is not, even he is the eighth, and is of the seven, and goeth into perdition.*

Seven fills up the church age – seven is all power. There will be seven super powers down through time, from the establishment of the world. Five of them, in John's day, had already passed. One was at that present time and when the other one comes *he must continue a short space*. This is the assassinated world leader that Satan will have resurrected. *The beast that was and is not* is the eighth, but of the seven. He was of the seven world powers before he was assassinated and resurrected.

God, through the Holy Spirit, is giving John a preview of things that will actually take place in the nineteenth chapter.

> *12. And the ten horns which thou sawest are ten kings, which have received no kingdom as yet; but receive power as kings one hour with the beast.*

This is a short-lived group of national leaders. They will share power with the world leader (first beast).

It is clear that the prophet Daniel received end-time prophecy. As we study Revelation we can see that John, at a later day, receives confirmation of things prophesied in the seventh chapter of Daniel.

> *13. These have one mind, and shall give their power and strength unto the beast.*
> *14. These shall make war with the Lamb, and the Lamb shall overcome them: for he is Lord of lords, and King of kings: and they that are with him are called, and chosen, and faithful.*

These leaders will make war against Christ, but will be overcome by the King of Kings and Lord of Lords.

> *15. And he saith unto me, The waters which thou sawest, where the whore sitteth, are peoples, and multitudes, and nations, and tongues.*

When we put anything before God, it is spiritual adultery. The people referred to here are not even pretending to abide by the teaching of God's Word. We become one with

God when we become a Christian – when we follow what He says. Anything else is adultery. It is like the children of Israel when they decided to worship the same idols their neighbors worshipped, but would not miss going to the temple. God wants faithfulness from His people.

> 16. And the ten horns which thou sawest upon the beast, these shall hate the whore, and shall make her desolate and naked, and shall eat her flesh, and burn her with fire.

The ten horns, meaning ten heads of nations, hate the false prophet (false religious system). They want to *make her desolate and naked...and burn her with fire.*

> 17. For God hath put in their hearts to fulfill his will, and to agree, and give their kingdom unto the beast, until the words of God shall be fulfilled.

In the Old Testament the Bible says God put it in Pharaoh's heart to do what he did against Moses and the Israelite people. We might say, "The poor man didn't have a chance if God put it in his heart." We have to understand that <u>we</u> make the decisions. God has given us the freedom to think, will, and choose. We must not say, God made me make this or that decision. God doesn't make us do anything. He simply makes it possible for us to obey Him or reject Him. He has given us that freedom. God gives these people freedom to think, will and choose. This is how we can understand what happened. God did not make Pharaoh do what he did. He made him free like He has made every other man. Pharaoh chose to let what God told him harden his heart. God wants these people to fulfill His will. They can choose to let it bring them closer to God or to let it drive them farther away from Him.

18. And the woman which thou sawest is that great city, which reigneth over the kings of the earth.

The *great city* will be the religious city of the world.

There is nothing that a political religious leader wants more than to control government. We have some religious leaders today that would like to dictate what the government should accept or reject. In the end time this is going to happen. One religious leader, the false prophet, will rule *the kings of the earth* and he will do that through the world leader. The capitol of the false prophet will be the city of Jerusalem. After chasing the Jews into the wilderness he will use the temple as headquarters.

CHAPTER 18

*1. And after these things I saw another angel come down
from heaven, having great power; and the earth was
lightened with his glory.*

This angel from heaven, having been given great power,
tells the people of the earth what is happening.

*2. And he cried mightily with a strong voice, saying,
Babylon the great is fallen, is fallen, and is become the
habitation of devils, and the hold of every foul spirit,
and a cage of every unclean and hateful bird.*

This angel speaks, with authority from God, saying the
false religious system has lost its power and has opened its
doors to evil spirits.

*3. For all nations have drunk of the wine of the wrath
of her fornication, and the kings of the earth have
committed fornication with her, and the merchants of
the earth are waxed rich through the abundance of her
delicacies.*

The Holy Spirit has revealed to John that the dragon,
world leader, and false prophet will require the people who

buy or sell to take their number. This will control industry and taxation. Nothing will operate without authority from the three in power. This verse says *all nations have drunk of the wine of the wrath of her fornication* – which, again, means false teaching, simply devised of men. There will still be religion, but not approved of God. It will be of the false prophet and will be put forth in such a way that many people will be deceived. They will not understand that they are following after something that is anti-God. Satan is the master deceiver and the false prophet will be a master deceiver, as well.

> *4. And I heard another voice from heaven, saying, Come out of her, my people, that ye be not partakers of her sins, and that ye receive not of her plagues.*

The plagues are about to come upon her. God makes one last plea – *come out of her my people.* It is never too late as long as we are alive. Even in the end time it will not be too late for the people that do not take the mark of the beast to heed the calling of God. They will have what God has given every person – an ability to think, a freedom of will, and a freedom of choice. God said be faithful to Me. He can deliver us from whatever this world may inflict upon us. If we are going to be a faithful follower of the Lord Jesus Christ we must study and obey His Word. We must know what the Holy Spirit has revealed in the Bible.

There are good people all over this earth. There are people everywhere with the right spirit. God has ordained that man preach the gospel. Let's not let Him down. There are people everywhere that will follow the gospel when it is made known to them. Let's draw them to the Lord Jesus Christ and His Word.

He says, *come out my people* – even in the end He will still be calling.

5. For her sins have reached unto heaven, and God hath remembered her iniquities.

The sins of the false religions system have reached to the heavens and God remembers her iniquities. We find in the book of Revelation that this false system existed before Christ came to this earth as a baby. In fact, it was the false religious system that killed the prophets. They hated every man that brought the Word of God to them. They said, "Look where you came from...and you are trying to tell us what to do?" The prophet of God said, "I am telling you what God says - I am trying to help you." What did the false religious system do to them? They killed them! They analyzed the men without analyzing what they said. We cannot make the mistake of analyzing an individual without analyzing his message. They were murderers. They not only murdered the prophets, but they murdered our Lord.

6. Reward her even as she rewarded you, and double unto her double according to her works: in the cup which she hath filled fill to her double.

God says, "Reward her double for what she has done."

7. How much she hath glorified herself, and lived deliciously, so much torment and sorrow give her: for she saith in her heart, I sit a queen, and am no widow, and shall see no sorrow.

Here we have the boastful words from this ecumenical system. They say, "With the power that we have, we will never want for anything."

8. Therefore shall her plagues come in one day, death, and mourning, and famine; and she shall be utterly burned with fire: for strong is the Lord God who judgeth her.

We see swift destruction as John has a preview of what is going to happen. God, through the Holy Spirit, says that destruction will come unexpectedly to them. The Lord God of heaven will judge the system.

9. *And the kings of the earth, who have committed forni-cation and lived deliciously with her, shall bewail her, and lament for her, when they shall see the smoke of her burning.*
10. *Standing afar off for the fear of her torment, saying, Alas, alas that great city Babylon, that mighty city! for in one hour is thy judgment come.*

The false religious system will no longer be able to help the rulers and businessmen of the earth that will have partaken of her teaching and will have helped her to stay in power. These people will not want to be connected with her and will quickly distance themselves from her.

11. *And the merchants of the earth shall weep and mourn over her; for no man buyeth their merchandise any more:*

Some people say that the computer is the beast. I do not agree with that, but I think the beast will use the computer. This system is already developed for total control of the earth. It is in place. The computer is not being used for that purpose right now which proves that it is not the beast. When the world leader is in power, he will use the system to identify everyone, to know whether they have the number stamped on their hand or forehead.

The merchants of the earth shall weep and mourn over her; for no man buyeth their merchandise any more – she will lose her power and control.

12. *The merchandise of gold, and silver, and previous stones, and of pearls, and fine linen, and purple, and silk, and scarlet, and all thyine wood, and all manner vessels of ivory, and all manner vessels of most previous wood, and of brass, and iron, and marble.*
13. *And cinnamon, and odours, and ointments, and frankincense, and wine, and oil, and fine flour, and wheat, and beasts, and sheep, and horses, and chariots, and slaves, and souls of men.*

Doesn't that cover it all? They will control every item bought and sold, from jewelry to the flour that makes bread.

14. *And the fruits that thy soul lusted after are departed from thee, and all things which were dainty and goodly are departed from thee, and thou shalt find them no more at all.*

When our Lord returns He will do away with this system.

15. *The merchants of these things, which were made rich by her, shall stand afar off for the fear of her torment, weeping and wailing.*

God is allowing the apostle John to see a preview of the falling system.

16. *And saying, Alas, alas that great city, that was clothed in fine linen, and purple, and scarlet, and decked with gold, and precious stones, and pearls!*

It will be a very, very wealthy system. Those who are rich will support it and will not want to see it come to an end.

17. *For in one hour so great riches is come to nought. And every shipmaster, and all the company in ships, and sailors, and as many as trade by sea, stood afar off,*
18. *And cried when they saw the smoke of her burning, saying, What city is like unto this great city!*
19. *And they cast dust on their heads, and cried, weeping and wailing, saying, Alas, alas that great city, wherein were made rich all that had ships in the sea by reason of her costliness! For in one hour is she made desolate.*

Who will be affected by the fall of this evil system? Those who are deceived by it...these are people who have not studied and rightly divided the Word of God. He requires more of us than just going to church and believing what someone else says.

The merchants who make money by buying and selling and those in the shipping and delivery business will all be affected. Their source of wealth will have come to an end. It will be quite a surprise...one day, total control of the world and the next day, no control. They will lament and mourn her death.

20. *Rejoice over her, thou heaven, and ye holy apostles and prophets; for God hath avenged you on her.*
21. *And a mighty angel took up a stone like a great millstone, and cast it into the sea, saying, Thus with violence shall that great city Babylon be thrown down, and shall be found no more at all.*
22. *And the voice of harpers, and musicians, and of pipers, and trumpeters, shall be heard no more at all*

in thee; and no craftsman, of whatsoever craft he be, shall be found any more in thee; and the sound of a millstone shall be heard no more at all in thee;

23. *And the light of a candle shall shine no more at all in thee; and the voice of the bridegroom and of the bride shall be heard no more at all in thee; for thy merchants were the great men of the earth; for by thy sorceries were all nations deceived.*

24. *And in her was found the blood of prophets, and of saints, and of all that were slain upon the earth.*

This is a system that has been guilty of apostasy since before Christ.

The remaining chapters of the book of Revelation are as plain as can be. I will not do a lot of commenting on them.

Chapter 19

*1. And after these things I heard a great voice of much
people in heaven, saying, Alleluia; Salvation, and
glory, and honour, and power, unto the Lord our God:*

God makes these people knowledgeable of what He
is going to do. They all say, *Alleluia; Salvation, and
glory, and honour, and power, unto the Lord our God.*
The bridegroom is waiting for the complete collection
of the bride. In the last chapter of Revelation, the Lord has a
great celebration with the bride.

*2. For true and righteous are his judgments: for he hath
judged the great whore, which did corrupt the earth
with her fornication, and hath avenged the blood of
his servants at her hand.*

Here is the beginning of the judgment that we have just
read about in the eighteenth chapter and the people in heaven
say God is righteous – He is judging the great whore.

*3. And again they said, Alleluia. And her smoke rose up
for ever and ever.*

> 4. *And the four and twenty elders and the four beasts fell down and worshipped God that sat on the throne, saying, Amen; Alleluia.*
> 5. *And a voice came out of the throne, saying, Praise our God, all ye his servants, and ye that fear him, both small and great.*
> 6. *And I heard as it were the voice of a great multitude, and as the voice of many waters, and as the voice of mighty thunderings, saying, Alleluia: for the Lord God omnipotent reigneth.*

The *many waters* are people who have been rescued from the earth.

> 7. *Let us be glad and rejoice, and give honour to him: for the marriage of the Lamb is come, and his wife hath made herself ready.*

Heaven is glad and rejoices. There is about to be the complete collection of saints from the earth, who make up the bride of Christ.

> 8. *And to her was granted that she should be arrayed in fine linen, clean and white: for the fine linen is the righteousness of saints.*

When we think of the righteousness of the saints of God, we think of the Holy Spirit breathed Word where He gives us instruction in righteousness.

I became a Christian because I believe I am an eternal being – which God made me. God tells us in the Bible that we have two choices...hell, where we will be tormented forever with fire and brimstone, or heaven, where we can live happily with Him forever and ever. For selfish reasons I choose to live with God. In His Word, God says He has a mission for me. Once He saves us, we have a mission – to be the salt of the earth, to teach His Word. As long as we live, this is our mission.

> 9. *And he saith unto me, Write, Blessed are they which are called unto the marriage supper of the Lamb. And he saith unto me, These are the true sayings of God.*
> 10. *And I fell at his feet to worship him. And he said unto me, See thou do it not: I am thy fellow-servant, and of thy brethren that have the testimony of Jesus: worship God: for the testimony of Jesus is the spirit of prophecy.*

Here, John makes the mistake of falling at the feet of one who is a spokesman for God. Even though this spiritual being is speaking for God, he does not allow himself to be looked upon as God.

> 11. *And I saw heaven opened, and behold a white horse; and he that sat upon him was called Faithful and True, and in righteousness he doth judge and make war.*
> 12. *His eyes were as a flame of fire, and on his head were many crowns; and he had a name written, that no man knew, but he himself.*
> 13. *And he was clothed with a vesture dipped in blood: and his name is called The Word of God.*
> 14. *And the armies which were in heaven followed him upon white horses, clothed in fine linen, white and clean.*

I believe the armies that follow the Lord Jesus Christ, when He comes back to this earth, are the redeemed of the earth up to that point in time. I think the Holy Spirit identifies them by saying they are *clothed in fine linen, white and clean.* The King's garments are dipped in blood.

War is dirty. When I was in the military the general wore dress clothes and we, of the lower rank, wore fatigues. We were to do the fighting. I notice the opposite here. Our Lord has on garments dipped in blood. He will do the fighting and His armies will follow Him in fine linen, white, and clean.

The fight is over for those who have gone to be with God. As Christians we look forward to the fight being over. We wrestle against evil on this earth – against spiritual wickedness. We can never let down our guard.

> 15. *And out of his mouth goeth a sharp sword, that with it he should smite the nations: and he shall rule them with a rod of iron: and he treadeth the winepress of the fierceness and wrath of Almighty God.*
> 16. *And he hath on his vesture and on his thigh a name written, KING OF KINGS, AND LORD OF LORDS.*
> 17. *And I saw an angel standing in the sun; and he cried with a loud voice, saying to all the fowls that fly in the midst of heaven, Come and gather yourselves together unto the supper of the great God;*

We have been reading about a preview of things to come. How it is happening. The angel *calls all the fowls that fly in the midst of heaven* and says you are about to have a great supper. What is the supper going to be?

> 18. *That ye may eat the flesh of kings, and the flesh of captains, and the flesh of mighty men, and the flesh of horses, and of them that sit on them, and the flesh of all men, both free and bond, both small and great.*

Regardless of rank, they will be gathered in this great battle.

19. And I saw the beast, and the kings of the earth, and their armies, gathered together to make war against him that sat on the horse, and against his army.

They get ready to make war against Christ and the armies He will bring with Him.

20. And the beast was taken, and with him the false prophet that wrought miracles before him, with which he deceived them that had received the mark of the beast, and them that worshipped his image. These both were cast alive into a lake of fire burning with brimstone.

Notice the world leader who, after being assassinated, has more power when he is brought back to life, and the false prophet, who has power to do miracles, will both be cast into the lake of fire and brimstone.

21. And the remnant were slain with the sword of him that sat upon the horse, which sword proceeded out of his mouth: and all the fowls were filled with their flesh.

Earlier we read how deep the blood will run – as deep as a horse's bridle. There will be a tremendous amount of bloodshed as they go up against the Lord Jesus Christ, the King of Kings, the Lord of Lords. They will have no power against Him – they will be slain. This is why God will call *all the fowls* to come to the supper. He will call them to a feast of kings, horses, and of them that sit on them, the flesh of captains, the flesh of all men that will have taken the mark of the beast...those who will have been deceived by the false prophet and the miracles he performs.

CHAPTER 20

1. And I saw an angel come down from heaven, having the key of the bottomless pit and a great chain in his hand.

The false prophet and the world leader will have been cast into the lake of fire, burning with brimstone. Where is the dragon? We are going to find out what Christ does with the dragon.

2. And he laid hold on the dragon, that old serpent, which is the Devil, and Satan, and bound him a thousand years,

Why doesn't He put the dragon in the same place as the false prophet and world leader? He will put him in a different place. Satan is not going to be bound forever, but he will be bound for a time.

3. And cast him into the bottomless pit, and shut him up, and set a seal upon him, that he should deceive the nations no more, till the thousand years should be fulfilled: and after that he must be loosed a little season.

4. *And I saw thrones, and they sat upon them, and judgment was given unto them: and I saw the souls of them that were beheaded for the witness of Jesus, and for the Word of God, and which had not worshipped the beast, neither his image, neither had received his mark upon their foreheads, or in their hands; and they lived and reigned with Christ a thousand years.*
5. *But the rest of the dead lived not again until the thousand years were finished. This is the first resurrection.*
6. *Blessed and holy is he that hath part in the first resurrection: on such the second death hath no power, but they shall be priests of God and of Christ, and shall reign with him a thousand years.*

...shall reign with Him a thousand years. During the thousand years there will be mortal and immortal beings (those who will return and reign with Christ) occupying the earth. It will be a peaceful time for the mortal beings because Satan and his influence will be gone for a thousand years.

7. *And when the thousand years are expired, Satan shall be loosed out of his prison.*
8. *And shall go out to deceive the nations which are in the four quarters of the earth, Gog and Magog, to gather them together to battle: the number of whom is as the sand of the sea.*

That will be a lot of people – *the number of whom is as the sand of the sea.* The only people Satan will be able to deceive are the mortals. He will have no power over the immortal people that live and reign with Christ on the earth. Satan will deceive many when he is *loosed a little season.*

9. *And they went up on the breadth of the earth, and compassed the camp of the saints about, and the beloved city: and fire came down from God out of heaven, and devoured them.*
10. *And the devil that deceived them was cast into the lake of fire and brimstone, where the beast and false prophet are, and shall be tormented day and night for ever and ever.*

Now God puts the devil (dragon) in the same place as the false prophet and the beast, to never be loosed again on mankind. That will be a wonderful day. As Christians, this is what we are looking forward to.

11. *And I saw a great white throne, and him that sat on it, from whose face the earth and the heaven fled away; and there was found no place for them.*
12. *And I saw the dead, small and great, stand before God; and the books were opened: and another book was opened, which is the book of life: and the dead were judged out of those things which were written in the books, according to their works.*

The dead, both small and great, stand before God and the books of the Old and New Testament will be opened.

13. *And the sea gave up the dead which were in it; and death and hell delivered up the dead which were in them: and they were judged every man according to their works.*
14. *And death and hell were cast into the lake of fire. This is the second death.*
15. *And whosoever was not found written in the book of life was cast into the lake of fire.*

If anyone thinks there is not a hellfire and brimstone religion to be taught, they had better read the Bible.

If I miss heaven (and I don't say that with uncertainty) it will not be God's fault. God has done all He will do for every soul on this earth. I will not miss heaven if I remain faithful to God.

Chapter 21

1. *And I saw a new heaven and a new earth: for the first heaven and the first earth were passed away; and there was no more sea.*

Some people say it is not totally unthinkable that God will refurbish this earth.

2. *And I John saw the holy city, new Jerusalem, coming down from God out of heaven, prepared as a bride adorned for her husband.*
3. *And I heard a great voice out of heaven saying, Behold, the tabernacle of God is with men, and he will dwell with them, and they shall be his people, and God himself shall be with them, and be their God.*
4. *And God shall wipe away all tears from their eyes; and there shall be no more death, neither sorrow, nor crying, neither shall there be any more pain: for the former things are passed away.*
5. *And he that sat upon the throne said, Behold, I make all things new. And he said unto me, Write: for these words are true and faithful.*
6. *And he said unto me, It is done. I am Alpha and Omega, the beginning and the end. I will give unto*

*him that is athirst of the fountain of the water of life
freely.*

7. *He that overcometh shall inherit all things; and I will
be his God, and he shall be my son.*

8. *But the fearful, and unbelieving, and the abominable,
and murderers, and whoremongers, and sorcerers,
and idolaters, and all liars, shall have their part
in the lake which burneth with fire and brimstone:
which is the second death.*

9. *And there came unto me one of the seven angels which
had the seven vials full of the seven last plagues, and
talked with me, saying, Come hither, I will shew thee
the bride, the Lamb's wife.*

The bride is the church that started to accumulate on the
day of Pentecost. This is the bride, the Lamb's wife, who
has special mentioning here and a special celebration in the
eternal order.

10. *And he carried me away in the spirit to a great and
high mountain, and shewed me that great city, the
holy Jerusalem, descending out of heaven from God,*

11. *Having the glory of God: and her light was like unto
a stone most precious, even like a jasper stone, clear
as crystal;*

12. *And had a wall great and high, and had twelve gates,
and at the gates twelve angels, and names written
thereon, which are the names of the twelve tribes of
the children of Israel:*

13. *On the east three gates; on the north three gates; on
the south three gates; and on the west three gates.*

14. *And the wall of the city had twelve foundations, and in
them the names of the twelve apostles of the Lamb.*

15. *And he that talked with me had a golden reed to measure the city, and the gates thereof, and the wall thereof.*

16. *And the city lieth foursquare, and the length is as large as the breadth: and he measured the city with the reed, twelve thousand furlongs. The length and the breadth and the height of it are equal.*

17. *And he measured the wall thereof, an hundred and forty and four cubits, according to the measure of a man, that is, of the angel.*

18. *And the building of the wall of it was of jasper: and the city was pure gold, like unto clear glass.*

19. *And the foundations of the wall of the city were garnished with all manner of previous stones. The first foundation was jasper; the second, sapphire; the third, a chalcedony; the fourth, an emerald;*

20. *The fifth, sardonyx; the sixty, sardius; the seventh, chrysolite; the eighty, beryl; the ninth, a topaz, the tenth, a chrysoprasus; the eleventh, a jacinth; the twelfth, an amethyst.*

21. *And the twelve gates were twelve pearls; every several gate was of one pearl: and the street of the city was pure gold, as it were transparent glass.*

22. *And I saw no temple therein: for the Lord God Almighty and the Lamb are the temple of it.*

23. *And the city had no need of the sun, neither of the moon, to shine in it: for the glory of God did lighten it, and the Lamb is the light thereof.*

24. *And the nations of them which are saved shall walk in the light of it: and the kings of the earth do bring their glory and honour into it.*

25. *And the gates of it shall not be shut at all by day: for there shall be no night there.*

26. *And they shall bring the glory and honour of the nations into it.*

27. And there shall in no wise enter into it any thing that defileth, neither whatsoever worketh abomination, or maketh a lie: but they which are written in the Lamb's book of life.

Here we have a description of the Holy city as it descends to the new earth. I emphasize the new earth. How big the new earth will be, we do not know. If we can interpret the measurements then we can know how big the Holy City will be – this will be our capitol. The splendor of it is described here. I certainly do look forward to seeing it.

The jewels mentioned were a part of the high priests garment in the Old Testament.

CHAPTER 22

1. *And he shewed me a pure river of water of life, clear as crystal, proceeding out of the throne of God and of the Lamb.*
2. *In the midst of the street of it, and on either side of the river, was there the tree of life, which bare twelve manner of fruits, and yielded her fruit every month: and the leaves of the tree were for the healing of the nations.*

Here on earth we do good to get one crop a year, but in the new economy there will be one crop a month. If you think we will not enjoy food there, think again. The eternal world will be without sin cursed conditions. There will be no hunger there. God will take care of our needs.

3. *And there shall be no more curse: but the throne of God and of the Lamb shall be in it; and his servants shall serve him:*

I read this verse at a funeral and afterwards someone said, "I caught that – there will be no more curse; that means there is a curse here, doesn't it?" I said, "Yes, we had this funeral today because we are living under sin cursed conditions."

4. *And they shall see his face; and his name shall be in their foreheads.*

5. *And there shall be no night there; and they need no candle, neither light of the sun; for the Lord God giveth them light: and they shall reign for ever and ever.*

6. *And he said unto me, These sayings are faithful and true: and the Lord God of the holy prophets sent his angel to shew unto his servants the things which must shortly be done.*

7. *Behold, I come quickly: blessed is he that keepeth the sayings of the prophecy of this book.*

I take this to mean the book of Revelation. *Blessed is he that keepeth the sayings of this book.*

8. *and I John saw these things, and heard them. And when I had heard and seen, I fell down to worship before the feet of the angel which shewed me these things.*

9. *Then saith he unto me, See thou do it not: for I am thy fellow-servant, and of thy brethren the prophets, and of them which keep the sayings of this book: worship God.*

10. *And he saith unto me, Seal not the sayings of the prophecy of this book: for the time is at hand.*

Seal not – a direct command from heaven to not seal up the prophecy of this book. How much plainer can it be? We say, "You must be baptized because God commands it." We must not seal up the prophecy of this book because God commands that we not do that. We cannot please God and seal it up.

11. He that is unjust, let him be unjust still: and he which is filthy, let him be filthy still: and he that is righteous, let him be righteous still: and he that is holy, let him be holy still.

The time is past for repenting. This is judgment day.

12. And behold, I come quickly; and my reward is with me, to give every man according as his work shall be.
13. I am Alpha and Omega, the beginning and the end, the first and the last.
14. Blessed are they that do his commandments, that they may have right to the tree of life, and may enter in through the gates into the city.

We have people in the world today that say we do not have to obey the commandments of God. They say He saves us by His grace. They say, "If we have to do the commandments of God we take away the grace." There is only one way we can find grace and favor with God and that is to keep His commandments, obey His Word, love and respect Him.

15. For without are dogs, and sorcerers, and whoremongers, and murderers, and adolaters, and whosoever loveth and maketh a lie.

Those who have not recognized God are the things mentioned in verse fifteen.

16. I Jesus have sent mine angel to testify unto you these things in the churches. I am the root and the offspring of David, and the bright and morning star.

Jesus is referring to the Holy Spirit message to the church of the Lord Jesus Christ.

17. And the Spirit and the bride say, Come. And let him that heareth say, Come. And let him that is athirst come. And whosoever will, let him take the water of life freely.

The angel is referring to the gospel and the bride, which is the church.

18. For I testify unto every man that heareth the words of the prophecy of this book, If any man shall add unto these things, God shall add unto him the plagues that are written in this book:
19. And if any man shall take away from the words of the book of this prophecy, God shall take away his part out of the book of life, and out of the holy city, and from the things which are written in this book.
20. He which testifieth these things saith, Surely I come quickly. Amen. Even so, come, Lord Jesus.
21. The grace of our Lord Jesus Christ be with you all. Amen

When you pray for knowledge, pick up your Bible and study. Do not give up. If we are persistent in our study, God will bless us with knowledge.

I can remember forty years ago when I said, "There is no way I can tackle that Bible." I prayed to God to give me the strength and determination to do it. I started to remember the scripture that says, *study to show thyself approved unto God, a workman that needeth not to be ashamed* (II Timothy 2:15). That was my answer – it did not come from a strange happening, it did not come from a dream, but it came from the Word of God. *Study to show yourself approved*. It has been the greatest blessing in the world for me.

Let's pray:

God, I thank you for this study. I thank you for these individuals, for their interest and their desire to know you. I pray for each and everyone, as well as myself. I ask your blessing upon us, that we may have a stronger desire, and will, to live for you and to be obedient to your Word, to make ourselves subject unto you. We want the blessings of eternal life and we want to live with you forever and ever. We pray for forgiveness of our sins – we pray in Jesus' name, Amen.

Printed in the United States
75344LV00002B/115-159